Transforming Feminist Practice

Non-Violence, Social Justice and the
Possibilities of a Spiritualized Feminism

by Leela Fernandes

Aunt Lute Books
San Francisco

First Edition

Aunt Lute Books
P.O. Box 410687
San Francisco, CA 94141

Cover Design, Text Design and Typesetting: Amy Woloszyn
Cover Art: Untitled. Mulberry paper, oranges, and wax (detail, digitally altered).
    Copyright © 2002 Cindy Cleary
Senior Editor: Joan Pinkvoss
Managing Editor: Shay Brawn
Production: Gina Gemello, Shahara Godfrey, Marielle Gomez, Tamara Martínez

This book was funded in part by grants from the California Arts Council and the National Endowment for the Arts.

Library of Congress Cataloging-in-Publication Data

Fernandes, Leela.
Transforming feminist practice : non-violence, social justice, and the possibilities of a spiritualized feminism / by Leela Fernandes.
p. cm.
Includes bibliographic references.
ISBN 1-879960-67-2
1. Feminism. 2. Social action. 3. Social justice. 4. Nonviolence. 5. Spirituality. I. Title.

HQ1154.F495 2003
305.42–dc21

Printed in the United States of America
10 9 8 7 6 5 4

ACKNOWLEDGMENTS

In writing this book, I benefitted and learned from many sources and individuals and I am grateful to all of them. For guidance at various points thanks go to Eileen, Carmen, Andrew and Clara. For friendship, support and needed distractions at different moments I am grateful to Ellie, Karen, Caridad, Ruthie, Laura, Jenn, Valerie, Brinda, Leslie, Sue and Prema. I am also grateful to Joan and Shay for their in-depth suggestions for revision and support of this book and to Gina for her careful editing. Responsibility for the arguments and ideas, of course, lies with me.

CONTENTS

Chapter 1 Introduction

An undergraduate class in Women's Studies in the United States culminates in a familiar scene. As in many Women's Studies classes, the course has spent fourteen weeks examining the complexities of women's lives, practices and attitudes in varying countries. Our discussions have spanned both large scale and local issues—the impact of global economic structures on women's daily lives, the ways in which such global structures interact with local inequalities in the family or community, and the ways in which hierarchies such as race, class, caste and gender intersect to shape the lives and identities of women. Students have responded with varying degrees of outrage, curiosity and indifference. Then a student throws up her hands and proclaims, "But these issues are too big to change. That's the way the system works." At this moment, a point that seems to arrive in every semester, even the most ardent progressive activists in the classroom will usually sit in awkward silence, tacitly agreeing, despite their most passionate arguments for social change during the course of the semester. The students seem to reach an unspoken understanding that all the issues we have dealt with and debated, the raging questions of how one thinks about, understands and ultimately transforms the intricate relations between different structures of inequality in local, national and international contexts have been nothing more than a fascinating learning experience. The work of the course has been simply a matter of theory, inapplicable in reality. At such moments, a curtain seems to have dropped, setting limits on the imagination of students. These largely self-selected students who are already interested in studying and confronting questions of social inequality and social change, these often deeply committed, passionate, bright young individuals who are or should be at the peak of idealism and hope for change, cannot find within themselves the means to simply imagine a world without hierarchy, exclusion or injustice.

At one level, this classroom scene appears to be no more than an ironic commentary on the closures endemic to twenty-first century society in a "new world order," one which has witnessed the apparent self-destruction of utopian ideologies such as socialism. At another level, these limits may appear to be due to the presumed economic privilege of college students in the United States.[1] Yet there is another possible explanation, one that has been often overlooked in conventional analyses of social and political life. This foreclosure of the imagination, I have come to believe, reflects a deeper spiritual crisis that often lurks behind visions of and movements for contemporary social justice.

Raising the question of spirituality may seem like an unlikely starting point at which to address concerns of social justice, particularly at the current moment. The rise of religious fundamentalist movements across the world has seemed more than ever to underline the immense importance of defining clear secular boundaries for contemporary visions of justice and order. Certainly, the attacks on women's and human rights which the Taliban perpetrated in Afghanistan provided a striking symbol of religious extremism in the Western imagination. While that image has unfortunately dovetailed with longstanding colonial misrepresentations of Islamic thought and life,[2] other cases, such as the gendered and racialized ideologies of Christian fundamentalism in the United States and attacks on religious minorities in India, have also provided important instances where firmly grounded secular responses have risen as the main responses for the protection of civil and human rights.

Given that public and politicized forms of spirituality have in recent decades come to be associated with conservative, patriarchal religious organizations and movements, the relevance of spirituality for social transformation has increasingly been rendered invisible. For instance, the significance of the deeper linkages between spirituality and social justice, linkages which were a cornerstone of the views of leaders such as Gandhi or Martin Luther King Jr., have for the most part not been given a central role in public historical memory and in the discourses and practices of new social movements. The loss of their original transformative understandings of the links between spirituality and social transformation has been accelerated due to two factors. On the one hand, nation-states have stepped in to iconize and appropriate the struggles of such leaders within state-oriented narratives of national progress. On the other hand, critics who have rightly sought to examine the limits and effects of the gender or class-based boundaries used by these movement leaders have paid less attention to the spiritual meaning of their practices. The net result has been a disruption of the connections between spirituality and social justice and a ceding of the space of spirituality to conservative religious and political forces.

There is no greater evidence of this than in mainstream feminist movements and theories. On the one hand, while feminists have rightly been wary of religious institutions that have sought to control women's bodies and sexualities, this wariness has inadvertently allowed conservative religious and political organizations and movements to colonize spirituality. On the other hand, the dissociation between spirituality and social justice has further alienated secular, urban, middle-class feminists from the majority of women whose understandings of their lives do not conform to easy distinctions between the secular and sacred.[3] At best, feminist theorists and organizations tend to relegate spirituality to the local "cultural" idioms of grassroots women (usually in "other" places and for "other" women), acknowledging it in the name of an uneasy cultural relativist tendency of "respecting cultural difference." Such an approach, however, misses the meanings and beliefs of a majority of the world's women who do not conceive of their relationship to their worlds, bodies and selves through modern notions of secularism; for such women, concepts of justice and equality and indeed of feminism are inextricably linked to notions of the sacred.[4]

Simply acknowledging these cultural differences as a supplement to feminism or seeing them as a problem for feminist outreach leaves feminism itself untouched. The question I want to explore in this book is one that pushes the boundaries of feminism a step further. I want to ask how feminist approaches to questions of social justice would change if the existing dichotomy between the material/political/social and the spiritual realms were to be set aside.[5] How would central feminist discussions of questions of identity, practice and knowledge be transformed? Furthermore, I want to argue that social transformation requires an explicit engagement with questions of spirituality.

When I speak of spirituality, at the most basic level I am referring to an understanding of the self as encompassing body and mind, as well as spirit. I am also referring to a transcendent sense of interconnection that moves beyond the knowable, visible material world. This sense of interconnection has been described variously as divinity, the sacred, spirit, or simply the universe. My understanding is also grounded in a form of lived spirituality, which is directly accessible to all and which does not need to be mediated by religious experts, institutions or theological texts; this is what is often referred to as the mystical side of spirituality. Rather than reacting to or trying to reform existing patriarchal religious traditions and structures,[6] this book is a reclaiming of this non-hierarchical, accessible understanding of spirituality.

Spirituality can be as much about practices of compassion, love, ethics and truth defined in non-religious terms as it can be related to the mystical reinterpretations of existing religious traditions.[7] Notions of divinity, in my understanding, are simultaneously immanent (residing within one's own self) and transcendent (which is understood by conventional religions through concepts of "God" but can just as easily be understood in terms of the universe).[8] In speaking of spirituality, divinity and the sacred, my aim is not to advocate a particular set of religious or theological beliefs. Nor is this book an argument for promoting a religious language for feminism or social justice movements, either for the strategic purpose of employing a language that can provide a more public or emotional appeal or for the purpose of respecting "different" cultural beliefs or ways of living. In effect, this book departs from conventional social and feminist analyses by taking the realms traditionally classified as the sacred, the spiritual, the divine and the mystical as real.

Reclaiming the sacred in this way is not simply a new linguistic or symbolic strategy for feminism. It goes to the heart of feminist struggles for social justice and can provide a critical foundation for social transformation. At one level, feminism becomes a means for the decolonization of the divine. At another level, the provision of spiritual strength to individuals deeply committed to social justice is more necessary than ever in a world racked by immense hatreds that feed on each other in endless cycles of retribution, always in the name of "justice." Finally, a spiritualization of social movements can provide a means with which to break from these cycles of retribution which perpetuate multiple and linked forms of oppression so that social movements continually find themselves appropriated by or circumscribed within the very structures they have tried wholeheartedly to resist.

This book is about the possibilities of spiritualized social transformation of this world, one that seeks to challenge all forms of injustice, hierarchy and abuse from the most intimate daily practices in our lives to the larger structures of race, gender, class, sexuality and nation. In contrast to strategic arguments which classify the spiritual as a language or tool to be deployed in order to mobilize masses for the "real" goals of social justice, I argue that movements for social justice are sacred endeavors. Furthermore, I suggest that movements for social or political transformation have faltered not because of the impossibility of realizing their visions of social justice, but because such transformations cannot be complete unless they are explicitly and inextricably linked to a deeper form of spiritual transformation on a mass basis. In a world marked by violent ethnic, racial and religious conflict and deepening social and economic inequality, any possibility of social transformation also requires a spiritual revolution, one which transforms conventional understandings of power, identity, and justice—understandings which are currently limited by a series of false distinctions between the spiritual and the material, the sacred and the secular, the human and the divine. A central argument of this book is that if movements for social justice are to be fully transformative, they must be based on an understanding of the connections between the spiritual and the material realms. History has shown us that progressive social movements that have rested on an assumption that the spiritual and material are opposed, or even disconnected, realms have ultimately tended to reproduce the kinds of power relations they have sought to change. For example, class-based labor movements in varying contexts have struggled with the ways in which they have often reproduced other forms of social oppression such as gender, race or ethnicity, while the well-intentioned attempts of Western feminists to speak on behalf of global women's oppression have often implicated them in colonial and racialized discourses that have stereotyped Third World countries as backward and oppressive.[9] My point in addressing such limitations is not to ignore or dismiss the invaluable struggles and accomplishments of such social movements. Rather my intention is to open up the space for the possibility of a more complete transformation, one that builds on the gains and insights of social movements and thought that address inequalities such as gender, class, race and nation. Leaving the contradictions of power and the subtle exclusions inherent in social movements and conceptions of social justice unexamined risks cynicism, despair and eventually the departure of those who are on the margins of subordinated groups.[10] In this endeavor, I explore the ways in which a specific focus on spirituality can aid in opening up such space and in transcending some of these contradictions of power. I specifically focus on the question of feminism, both in terms of feminist practice and contemporary feminist thought.

Contemporary feminism provides a particularly fruitful place for the exploration of broader questions of social justice because of the ways in which feminists have sought to address multiple forms of structural inequality such as race, nation, class and sexuality, in addition to gender issues. It is in this broader sense of the social transformation of all forms of social inequality that I define the boundaries of feminism.[11] I thus use feminism and social justice as interchangeable throughout this book. The critical discussions in which I engage in this book will, I hope, be read as a sign of the possibilities, rather than the limitations, of transformation that are inherent in feminist movements and approaches to knowledge.

I examine the ways in which some of the central debates and issues which have concerned feminist activist-thinkers would be transformed through an approach that connects questions of spirituality and social justice. Thus, I examine the politics of identity, the meaning of feminist practice, the relationship between theory and practice, and the possibilities of creating transformative kinds of knowledge. While I point to the limits of some existing approaches to feminism, I build on a range of existing feminist writings, particularly those by feminists of color in the U.S. and non-Western feminists. In the process, I draw on examples from both contemporary and historical global political events. I also relate my arguments to my teaching in Women's Studies; in many ways this book is a product of my engagement, frustrations and learning from the students who have come my way during the past ten years of teaching about feminism. By addressing this range of examples, I seek to disrupt any notions of a presumed distinction or dichotomy between feminist social activism and practices in the academy. Both are political and social sites which I draw on in order to examine the implications and possibilities of a spiritualization of feminist thought and practice.

To raise the possibility of spiritualizing feminism is in many ways to propose an uneasy task because of a long history in which the invocation of God, divinity and the sacred have become associated with violence and oppressions. This history, in which numerous wars have been fought and forms of social oppression justified "in the name of God," has led to the secularized visions of many social movements which struggle against various forms of inequality and oppressions.[12] Certainly there is no better example of this than feminist or women's movements that have seen time and again the ways in which culture or religion have been used to justify the oppression of women. The secularization of feminism has in many ways been necessary, as have many governmental policies of secularism. This book is not a theoretical or political attack on either feminist or state secularism. The displacement of questions of spirituality is more than understandable given the ways spirituality has been appropriated by states and conservative political movements. However, the results of this displacement have served to curtail the potential of women's movements and activism. Not only has this represented lost symbolic and material ground for such movements, it has also allowed these colonizing forces to pervert and distort the deeply egalitarian visions of truth and justice which lie at the mystical core of different spiritual traditions. In that sense, the spiritualization of feminism does not simply entail a one-way process of rethinking the boundaries of feminism through a spiritualized perspective, it also entails a taking back of the realms of the sacred from those forces that have sought to distort divinity or spirituality into a means for the reproduction of hierarchy, oppression and exclusion of subordinated social groups.

Individuals and groups absorbed in current conflicts often operate with the deep-seated belief that they are engaged in a sacred practice sanctioned by their religious/spiritual convictions for a divine cause. This belief cuts across political and ideological differences. Certainly Western representations have focused on the Islamic "holy war." However, such convictions also underlie the actions of individuals who support Hindu nationalist causes in India, for instance, as in the destruction of the Babri Masjid mosque and the campaign to build a temple at Ayodhya in the alleged site of the birthplace of Ram; they also characterize the beliefs of many citizens and political leaders in the United States who implicitly or explicitly believe that the start of a war against terrorism is a divinely ordained act in the fight of good and evil.[13] Secular critics have paid a great deal of energy in arguing that such cases are instances where leaders manipulate religion for other ends, and certainly such religious leaders have very clear "secular" desires for political power.

However, in addition to understanding such beliefs in terms of interests and ideology, progressive activists and intellectuals must understand the ways in which beliefs in the divine or moral foundations of acts based on violence, oppression and division distort spirituality, violating the mystical teachings of the very religious traditions being invoked, a viewpoint which is often overlooked. What do calls for terror in the name of an Islamic holy war have to do with the mystical Islamic teachings of Sufism, which ask us to "be in this world but not of this world," and which ask us to live sacred lives that are completely disidentified with materialistic worldly pursuits? How does a conception of a militant Hinduism which asserts an attachment to Hindu identity reconcile itself with the teachings of the Bhagavad Gita that ask us to free ourselves from the bonds of attachment, desire and identification? How does an imperialistic Christian belief in divine retribution with its advocacy of the use of violence against the evils of the "uncivilized" world reconcile itself with Christ's message of a radical egalitarian love of one's enemies? Such spiritual teachings point to a sacred, radical vision of social justice which is fundamentally opposed to any hierarchical, patriarchal or violent representations of religious teaching. These mystical ideas hold within them a vision of a transformative form of egalitarianism that can be put into practice in this world. Such truths do not rest on an otherworldly utopia or heaven. They are premised on a confrontation with and dissolution of the deepest forms of division and hierarchy which are at the root of all of forms of oppression *in this world*. Put into practice, this mystical knowledge can provide an unshakable foundation for movements for social justice.

I propose in this book that nothing short of a spiritual revolution will enable us to begin to manifest our visions of social justice, equality and transformation. Individuals and groups concerned with struggles against all forms of inequality and oppression have the potential within them to transform the meaning and practice of spirituality.[14] There is an historic moment now where individuals, regardless of their own personal backgrounds, are beginning to see the interconnections of a fully globalized world; writers and activists have increasingly moved away from older models of social change that focus on single issues to coalition work and to a deeper understanding of the interconnections between what appear to be separate structures of oppression. In the United States, for instance, a number of feminist writers and activists have addressed the interconnections between all social hierarchies, such as those based on gender, class, race, nation and sexuality.[15] In this endeavor, it is critical that we understand that a transformation of such vast structures of inequality must also simultaneously engage in a transformation of spirituality within this world.

In a world where spirituality is continually appropriated by exclusionary and hierarchical structures, any movement for social justice must also encompass within it a movement to produce alternative understandings of spirituality that can begin to break down the artificial barriers which religious orders have created in the name of theological purity and can firmly articulate a vision of spirituality that is linked to material transformation in this world. For too long now, spirituality has been associated with the belief that this world is a kind of waiting room for the real utopia that we must aspire to attain. This belief rests on the same kind of material-spiritual dichotomy which secular thinkers have put forth and which ironically has persisted, despite the very real material effects that different spiritual beliefs and religious orders have had throughout history. In fact, the utopias which mystics have spoken of must be made here, in this world. To believe otherwise, I suggest, is to attempt to escape the social and spiritual responsibility each of us has been given with life.

This kind of spiritual revolution also transforms significant aspects of existing approaches to feminism and social justice. Each of the following chapters, "Identity," "Practice," "Knowledge" and "Spirituality," explores an important locus of existing feminist practice, asking in each instance how a spiritualized feminism might help us to overcome the impasses we find there. I begin with the question of identity because identity has been a crucial arena which feminists and social activists have both criticized as a basis for oppression and used as a basis for mobilization. I argue in chapter 2, "Identity," that feminist movements for social justice will need to fundamentally break with political and social visions that rest on bounded bases of identification (such as gender and race), with conceptions of justice linked to retribution for past injustices and with attempts to gain power which are bound to inevitably reproduce the very structures that these movements struggle against. A spiritualized approach can enable this break from an identity-based framework. Such an approach is based on a recognition of the spiritual responsibility that each individual holds in processes of social change—a responsibility which, unlike conservative discourses of "personal responsibility," confronts the fundamental linkages between self-examination, self-transformation and individual ethical action on the one hand, and the transformation of larger structures of oppression on the other hand.

This sense of responsibility has numerous meanings and layers of significance for the possibilities of building an egalitarian and peaceful society. The central basis of my approach to the spiritualization of social justice is the philosophy and practice of non-violence. In chapter 3, "Practice," I use an exploration of the philosophy of non-violence to rethink existing feminist approaches to activism, drawing on examples from both well-known and less visible examples of non-violent activism, as well as from the work of feminist writer-activists who have engaged in what Gloria Anzaldúa and Jacqui Alexander have called a form of "spiritual activism;"[16] that is, a form of activism that works to transform all structures of hierarchy and exclusion and is based on a spiritualized understanding of ourselves both as individuals and as part of a larger interconnected world.

A philosophy of non-violence requires a rethinking of existing conceptions of power and justice. Recent thinkers and social theorists have cautioned us against viewing power as a tool or weapon or resource that can be seized or used over someone. Michel Foucault, for instance, has explained that power is more like a network of small capillaries running throughout society and producing our behaviors, attitudes and selves (1978; 1980). Power, as Foucault noted, cannot simply be partitioned off and wielded as a weapon to restrain and repress because it is an infinite field—it runs through and within us, constituting our very beings. What thinkers building on Foucault's work have stopped short of, however, is the possibility of transforming the definition of power in ways which reach beyond the material realm (whether that materiality is defined in an economic, discursive or cultural sense). The possibilities of spiritual power are usually missing in both modern and postmodern views. In modern understandings, power is a negative force used to control and dominate others. In postmodern approaches, although power is productive (it produces behaviors and identities) its presence is still implicitly continuing, and there is little space for broader social transformation that can change the way it works. Both views treat power as something that is limiting and which is interchangeable with control.[17]

For too long now, gaining control has been synonymous with ending the exploitation of marginalized social groups.[18] Social justice movements have historically based their struggles on the sometimes implicit premise that they are fighting for one's rights, for taking back what has been stolen, for getting back one's control—whether over resources or, more fundamentally, over one's life. Social movements have usually concentrated on making demands on external material sources such as the state, the law or institutions. While such demands have often been important and are a necessity in making changes in the material lives of some groups or individuals, the exclusive focus on a narrowly defined material realm has ultimately locked most social movements into a series of oppositional struggles which have trapped subordinated groups into demands for limited kinds of power and equality. Such struggles have focused primarily on making demands for limited kinds of resources like wages, access to jobs and equal treatment under the law. This is in no way intended to dismiss the important accomplishments, intentions or courage which many individuals and movements have shown in their struggles for equality and justice; nor is it to dismiss the necessity of struggles for material equality. However, even the most victorious of such struggles have only been and, I suggest, can only be partial. When one group has gained economically, another has taken its place at the bottom of the hierarchy. As some women have benefitted from the women's movement and have moved on to better jobs and better wages others have been trapped at the bottom of the ladder, cleaning their floors as they focus on breaking glass ceilings. As some groups have struggled for civil rights and access to the full privileges of citizenship, others have been placed in permanent liminal places as "undocumented" workers in sweatshops.[19] In fact, a preoccupation with the view that social justice exclusively involves making gains for specific groups has concealed the possibility that a lasting transformation of society can never rest on a movement based purely on making demands, on an ideology of getting more—no matter how just these demands may be. I explore in chapter 3 the possibilities of an approach to feminism that is simultaneously committed to processes of both making demands and of giving up.

What then would such a spiritualized form of transformation look like? What, for instance, would a social movement such as a women's movement or a labor movement based on a spiritualized vision of *this world* look like? How would we need to transform our understandings of ideas such as "resistance," "revolution," and of "justice"? My goal is not to provide a finite set of answers to these questions but to open up the space for ongoing contemplation and practice. These are not theoretical questions for philosophers to debate within the walls of ivory towers. For too long now the distinction between theory and practice has produced anguish amongst students who then struggle to bridge the gap. The practice and philosophy of nonviolence, as I will argue, belies any possible distinction between the two. The assumed divide between theory and practice only exists because of a deep alienation of the spirit. In practice we live, indeed we enact, what seem like abstract concepts such as justice, structural oppression, social change and transformation in every moment of our lives, in every relationship, from the most mundane interactions we engage in with strangers in supermarkets to the most intimate relationships we have with loved ones to the most public interactions we have in work, school, society, the world. The concepts that we think through, the limits and possibilities of the worlds we can imagine—these seemingly abstract questions are as real as the most tangible of protests or organizations we may wish to join or support.

I began this chapter by commenting on the inability of many students I have taught to even imagine another possibility for the ways we can live our lives. The most ardent feminist advocates speaking out against inequalities of race, class and gender will inevitably say that this can only be a theoretical discussion. And so it is that the imagined alternative is cordoned off safely from the world of practice, a partitioning that then enables us to avoid the responsibility for changing our lives and our worlds. Students' resistance to things they deem too abstract and theoretical is not merely a reaction to theories that seem too elitist or overly complex. Rather, I have found that such resistances often represent a fear of having to engage in the arduous and often painful process of self-transformation. Utopias are inconvenient because they necessitate deep-seated changes in ourselves and in the ways in which we live our lives. The irony here is that such "theoretical" utopias require *labor*.

A central part of this labor involves the creation of transformative forms of knowledge. Recent postmodern approaches in feminist scholarship and social theory have already provided important understandings that address the links between power and knowledge—the ways in which the forms of knowledge we produce are constitutive of unequal relationships of power and have real material effects that serve to marginalize and colonize subordinated groups. Yet in many ways the depth of such theoretical insights has in itself proved to be insufficient in producing a vision of transformative knowledge. If such work continually points to the often violent limits of the knowledge that is produced, it has stopped short of giving us an alternative form of knowledge that can transcend these limits. If such work has demonstrated the ways in which the search for "truth" has in reality engaged in a production of a truth that serves to justify, if not bolster, unequal relationships of power, it has stopped short of recognizing that larger truths which transcend the limited forms we have produced *do exist*.[20]

The problem is, postmodern thinkers have given us all of the tools to criticize and interrogate the deepest and largest structures of power—patriarchy, colonialism, capitalism, to name a few—and then told us that we can never escape these structures, that there is no way to transcend the spirals of power and knowledge. Such an approach simply produces closures for students and individuals who have the passion and the will to change this world. The psychic and physical frustrations of this feeling of being trapped by the enormity of the global systems of power inevitably lead many to an anger at those who have shown us the ways in which all aspects of our lives, from our deepest knowledge structures to the most mundane of cultural forms such as films and television shows, are fundamentally implicated in these systems of power.

In an attempt to find ways beyond this paralysis I explore in chapter 4, "Knowledge," the transformative possibilities of extending the practice of non-violence to the realm of knowledge. In the academy, insights and possibilities for social transformation are often trapped by ego-related attitudes and claims regarding the ownership of truth (even while postmodern tendencies within the academy deny the existence of truth). These attitudes ironically mirror the approaches of the religious orders and hierarchies which secular thinkers have rebelled against. Both sides lay claim to an ownership of truth and knowledge, and then sit in apprehensive judgment of those they deem lesser in some form; the result is the colonization of truth and the creation of an edifice of power, control and privilege. As an alternative, I address the possibilities of treating knowledge as a sacred process of witnessing, rather than as a commodity to be bought and sold in a marketplace.

The very idea of mystical knowledge has been all but absent in most feminist discussions. Yet it is precisely this absence that a great deal of feminist thought has implicitly sought to fill. Indeed all of the expansive feminist scholarship which has pointed to the partiality of the knowledge we produce within the constraints of our institutions, which has questioned the notion of objectivity, which has struggled to preserve links between knowledge and social justice, which has enabled forms of writing where it is legitimate to insert ourselves, our visions, our emotions, our conscience and our heart; all of this in many ways has been a kind of collective struggle and plea for a space where we are allowed to write with spirit. In fact, most grassroots movements for social justice, whether they are secular or not, embody within them a deeper spiritual knowledge of transformation and egalitarianism in this world.[21]

However, spirituality does not represent a realm that is innocent or naturally free from questions of power. If movements for social justice can be transformed through an engagement with spirituality, spirituality must also be transformed through the egalitarian visions that feminists and social activists are committed to. We are at a place in history where the mention of spirituality may be likely to conjure up images of right-wing fundamentalism or a quirky "New Age" fantasy. Such images point to the ways in which spirituality has been curtailed into a force that either seeks to evade or reproduce material inequalities. In chapter 5, "Spirituality," I confront such issues and argue for a process of decolonization of the divine, a process that can transform the relationships of power that are often encoded in existing understandings of spirituality.

My hope in writing this book is thus to open up possibilities that can transcend the careful fences that have cordoned off the spiritual and the material realms of knowledge and activism. Such possibilities require an approach that allows for a spiritualization of all of the territories that have been bounded through claims of ownership, always made in the name of justice—power, resistance, identity, knowledge, activism. It is at this space that lies at the crossroads of spirituality and social justice that I want to locate this book. I write this book at a time when the world is embedded in a global wave of violence, war and repression on an unprecedented scale and in a way in which no group of people within this world will be left untouched. It is perhaps an ironic moment to speak of social transformation, as individuals and groups that have dedicated their lives to peace, anti-discrimination and egalitarianism are increasingly on the defensive, at a time when it will take all of our resources to curtail even a portion of the violent forms of repression that are being unleashed. In a world with such escalating violence and poverty, where no individual, group or nation can find a protective bubble within which to isolate itself from connection and responsibility to the rest of the world, survival itself now seems linked to an ability to imagine a world completely transformed and free from all forms of inequality, prejudice, hatred and ignorance. But this book is not about the imagination. Indeed the imagination is only a thin layer, the outer skin of our deepest spiritual selves. Striking at and igniting the imagination produces a spark within us. However, the kind of transformation that is needed now will require a fire burning from our deepest sources of spiritual strength and knowledge.

Now more than ever it is critical to recognize that the potential for a non-violent transformation of this world is real, no matter how pejorative the word "utopia" may appear given the global social, political and economic circumstances that shape the dawn of the twenty-first century. It is now more than ever that we need to forge new paths for a spiritual revolution—paths that will finally decolonize spirituality from the religious hierarchies that claim and manipulate it for their own interests and that will produce transformative movements that are no longer forced to mirror the very structures of power they seek to change. It is in this spirit of working to open up such space that I offer the following reflections on politics, feminism, spirituality and social justice.

Social identity has been a central area which activist-thinkers have both embraced as a means to mobilize subordinated groups and rejected as an exclusionary basis of social hierarchies. The paradoxical nature of identity is perhaps one of the most significant and most difficult issues which we continue to navigate. In many ways, the social nature of identity—the affiliations of individuals with larger social groups and the cultural attributes which individuals and groups use to define and name themselves—has provided one of the most fertile grounds for contemporary thought and political activity. The politics of identity, for instance, has taken many different forms. States have defined identities and imposed them on individuals and groups (for example, through racial and ethnic classifications) in order to facilitate control of their civilian populations. Dominant groups have used social and cultural forms of identification in order to preserve their material privileges and exclude other social groups. Social movements in turn have used identity to reverse such exclusions. Women's movements have used identity-based claims to press for women's rights. Subordinated and marginalized ethnic and racial groups have seized on the notion of identity to mobilize around structural inequalities which have excluded them from economic, political and social resources and institutions.

Meanwhile, in the academy, identity has served as an often deeply polarizing subject. Writers and scholars have emphasized the politics of gender, racial and ethnic identities as a strategy for promoting gender and racial/ethnic diversity amongst students and teachers, and for expanding multicultural education. That effort, however, has often been met by a political backlash against "identity politics," finding support amongst individuals and groups on both the left and right of the ideological spectrum. On the right, multicultural education has posed a threat to dominant views of what texts and perspectives represent "real" knowledge.[1] Meanwhile on the left, individuals have often viewed the focus on identity as a distraction from socio-economic, class-based approaches to politics.[2] Ironically, marginalized individuals and groups who have called attention to inequalities based on identities such as race, gender and sexuality have often been accused of merely attempting to gain privileges or market their own identities. Too often, such backlashes are rooted in the economic and institutional interests of dominant groups being destabilized by the entry of "new" groups with their own visions of knowledge, politics and society. This is perhaps most evident in the recent attacks on affirmative action. Critics of affirmative action have misrepresented it as giving privileges to groups who are discriminated against; in other words, the correction of inequality is presented as privilege. In fact, these backlashes themselves simply indicate another set of identity politics—dominant groups holding on to their own carefully crafted territories. Thus, the politics of identity has persisted with an unceasing force and in often unseen ways both inside and outside the academy.

Indeed, the weight of identity has perhaps never been more clear than in recent events unfolding after the terrorist attacks against the World Trade Center and Pentagon in the United States. The reduction of the identity of terrorists to those who look "Middle Eastern" or, in the worst forms of mainstream television news reporting, those who look "Arabic," has soaked through the American nation-state. Immediately following the attacks, news reports even presented, with an indelible sense of relief, interviews with African Americans and Latinos who admitted to being afraid of Middle Eastern men in public spaces. Racial profiling, such media representations seem to want to say, is not after all a problem of white perception of dark skins, it is a national endeavor now aimed at the defense of the country. However, despite this divide-and-rule approach to the politics of race, the current culture of security has redeployed older practices of racialization in the construction of foreigners as terrorists. While such strategies have targeted Arab and Muslim men (for example through secret detentions and the enforced registration of specific groups of non-immigrant Muslim men) the war against terror has also returned to more generalized racial fears, for example by invoking older anxieties about illegal immigrants crossing the U.S.-Mexico border. The borders between white Americans and immigrants of color are being cemented in new ways as darkness becomes once again an unmistakable sign of threat and violence, both a symbolic and physical threat to what politicians, news commentators and civilians alike identify as "our way of life." Innocent individuals who may "look wrong" to others already stand accused of their identity. Such examples, needless to say, underline the fact that identity matters.

The problem that identity poses for activists/thinkers is that it presents a paradox in the struggle for social justice. That is, identity is a real material force in producing exclusion and hierarchy that cannot simply be wished away. Critics who dismiss movements that focus on identity-based exclusions as a diversionary or personalized form of "identity politics" fail to recognize the structural nature of identity. However, identity cannot, as I will argue, provide an adequate political basis for lasting social transformation. Identity-based movements, while effective for short-term political or material gains, end up with restricted constituencies and visions of social justice. Such restrictions ultimately serve as an obstacle to social transformation. The debate on identity thus often becomes polarized between those who deny material inequalities based on identity on the one hand, and those who support an oppositional form of identity politics which ultimately cannot move beyond the limits of particular identity groupings on the other.

Let us consider this paradox further. Identity represents a structuring force in society that states and dominant social groups actively use to produce various forms of inequality. That is, throughout history, dominant groups have used different forms of social identity to create material hierarchies that have systematically excluded other groups from access to economic resources, political rights and social and cultural equality. Such processes are structural because they become rigid and lasting forms of hierarchy that restrict choices and opportunity in enduring ways. For example, racial identity in the United States shapes the ways the economy is structured since subordinated racial groups such as African Americans and Latinos have historically received differential access to education, jobs and other kinds of economic resources.[3] Globally, identities such as gender, caste and ethnicity operate in similar kinds of ways. Given the structural nature of this process, activists committed to social justice cannot simply dismiss identity as a form of personal or cultural affiliation. Progressive critics who have argued against identity-based approaches to politics have often overlooked this. They have mistakenly used the term "identity politics" in ways that have confused struggles against social inequality with symbolic demands for a more personal or individualized form of recognition.[4]

Currently, with divisions of race, ethnicity and nation drawn in such firm and rigid ways, it is perhaps not surprising that so many have fallen back into a defensive protection of identity as a strategy of survival and resistance. In response to the material exclusions of identity, writers and activists have used identity as a tool to analyze social inequality and as basis for mobilization. In many instances, such responses have taken the form of an oppositional politics, in which subordinated groups have seized on the identity (as workers, women, African Americans, Asians, immigrants) which served to enforce their subordination and utilized it as a basis for political mobilization. This has produced important and necessary social movements which have made significant strides in addressing various forms of inequality in specific contexts. However, while identity-based movements are effective in mobilizing short term political action, in the long run they cannot produce an alternative future that is free from the very identity-based divisions and inequalities that they oppose. The problem here is a slippage that occurs between the need to understand how identity produces hierarchies and exclusions that shape social, economic and political life, and the political responses that are developed to transform such processes. While oppositional movements and discourses based on identity have been necessary to address the blindness to various forms of injustice, such movements cannot in the long run provide a viable alternative because they inevitably must rest on a form of identification that explicitly or implicitly is based on an oppositional distinction from another group. It is this sense of distinction (or sense of otherness) that is the underlying foundation of inequality and exclusion.

My intention here is not to reproduce attacks which have become customary in mainstream culture as well as in the ideological polemics on both the right and the orthodox left. These attacks usually dismiss or underplay the material and social effects of identity-based inequalities.[5] On the contrary, as I have noted, identity matters—in producing economic inequalities and structures in differing historical and national contexts; in excluding groups and individuals from access to political resources and institutions; in defining which groups count as legitimate citizens in both democratic and non-democratic political systems; and, finally, in shaping political attitudes, responses and resistances to such boundaries and exclusions.[6] I argue that while the very real hierarchies and exclusions of identity must be confronted and changed, the politics of identity cannot provide a lasting strategy for transformative social justice. Instead, in this chapter I discuss the possibilities of an alternative approach to social change—one that builds on a process of disidentification. Disidentification, as I will illustrate, is a twofold process. At one level, it rests on a letting go of all attachments to externalized forms of identity as well as to deeper ego-based attachments to power, privilege and control. At another level, disidentification is not simply a negative process of detachment but a positive movement of creating a different form of self. This disidentified form of self draws on a spiritualized perspective that does not need to resort to the traps, limitations and temporary security of identity. As I hope to demonstrate, this process of disidentification is not simply a theoretical exercise in imagining a different kind of self but a practical process for thinking about a different basis from which to work for real struggles for social justice.

THE PROBLEM OF IDENTITY

The problem of identity is not something that can be easily dismissed. Even a quick glance at any current newspaper will unfortunately reveal the enduring power of identity. In many ways, identity remains the central means by which individuals and groups attempt to create a sense of security in the midst of a fast paced, ever-changing world. This link between identity and security holds true for both dominant and subordinated forms of identity. Consider, for instance, the widespread displays of American flags by individuals in the aftermath of the 9/11 terrorist attacks. The strength of post-9/11 nationalist sentiments are a perfect example of a highly visible, dominant form of identification. While there may be clear differences in the motivations for flying the flag (immigrant business owners may, for instance, fly the flag strategically as a form of symbolic protection against violent hate crimes), the symbolic act is a form of identification in response to high levels of anxiety and insecurity. Critics who view this act only as an aggressive form of American nationalism, I believe, miss the ways in which the act is simultaneously a fear-driven grasp for security, based on the mistaken notion that security can be grounded in an external, material form of identification.

The fact that nationalist identification creates a false sense of safety through exclusion and defensiveness is usually clear for individuals committed to social justice. However, the issue which has been more difficult to address is the fact that a similar analysis can be applied to forms of identification which have the goal of social justice, such as the feminist identification with women or racial, ethnic and sexual minorities mobilizing around the identities that function to subordinate them (black, queer, Latino).[7] For such groups, identity continues to serve as the ground from which to work for change and to which to retreat for a sense of safety and belonging. Consider the ways in which identification has operated in debates on the nature of feminism. The process of identification that operates in feminist movements has historically rested on the assumption that women are bonded by their identities *as women*. This has posed a number of problems for feminists. For example, relationships of power and inequalities between women must always be raised as a challenge to this presumed identification; difference in this framework is by definition secondary and therefore always potentially divisive. The persistence of what Norma Alarcón has called the "logic of identification"[8] continues to serve as an underlying foundation for feminism. While such problems have been discussed at length by feminist writers and activists, this process of identification has not been dislodged in practice. This is clearly illustrated in the practice of teaching about feminism. Despite all of the advances in feminist understandings of identity, the presumption that students taking a class on feminism usually make is that women are connected by their social identities *as women*. The significance of identity is further underlined in the classroom because social identities are the key tools which students grasp at to make sense of their world, their politics and their visions of justice.

There are two central problems with the ways this emphasis on identity unfolds in the classroom. First, I have found in my own experiences of teaching that challenges to the naturalness of women's unity produces a defensive reaction from some students. This defensiveness is usually linked to a fear on the part of students as they begin to feel uncomfortably implicated in seemingly large and impersonal structures of inequality such as racism and colonialism, by virtue of their own social locations of racial, class and national privilege in the contemporary United States. In other words, one of the main difficulties of teaching about these issues is that the students' resistance to addressing such questions often stems from an implicit identification with the structures and privileges being questioned even as they claim that they want to transcend them. What I mean by this is that the confrontation of one's own personal privilege only produces resistance or discomfort if one identifies with or is attached in some way to that privilege. The second problem is that students who do want to address such privilege also often revert to identity-based approaches. For instance, students of color may defensively fall back onto claims that their racial and ethnic identities are a source of authentic knowledge.[9] This once again places these students into the confines of a rigid identity group which cannot account for differences, including ideological differences, between students of color and which does not ultimately disrupt the underlying logic of identification. This example is of course not unique to the classroom; nor is it unique to feminism. It reflects a much deeper problem that writers and activists continue to struggle with.

Many feminists have attempted to break from such frames of power by producing new forms of language that point to the shifting, fluid, contextual, multiple and intersecting identities that define individuals and groups.[10] Even with such efforts, however, the central approaches in feminism continue to rest on the logic of identification. Consider, for example, the implications of many of the challenges of feminists of color, lesbian feminists and postmodern feminists to the a priori assumption that women necessarily share common interests or attitudes. Such challenges have provided crucial understandings of the ways in which systems such as racial inequality and heterosexuality produce relationships of power between women. The result has been a move away from a gender-based approach to feminism to a focus on the ways in which gender must be understood in relation to identities such as race, class and sexuality. Yet while such insights have been crucial for the development of a more broad-based form of feminism, they have not been able to dislodge an identity-based approach to feminism. For instance, challenges of feminists of color have been mistakenly framed as identity claims even when such challenges have sought to dislodge identity as a fixed basis for feminist thought and action.[11] In other words, feminism has been broadened by including new identity groups of women—feminists of color, Third World feminists, lesbian feminists, working-class feminists—but such a framework of inclusion remains within an identity-based approach. AnaLouise Keating points to the limits of such an approach when she talks about the ways in which even challenges to hierarchies and stereotypes within feminism get trapped within identity-based structures. She asks, "What happens, once you're visible, once you have your new label(s)? Do you isolate yourself, splinter off into your own comforting home until internal conflicts arise and you begin recognizing differences between yourself and others who seem to share your label?"[12] The splintering that Keating describes underlines the false security of an identity-based approach to politics and knowledge; it is unable to rupture the fetters of identities which are placed on us (and which we place on ourselves) and which we are socialized to believe are necessary for our processes of self-definition.

The problem is that while identity-based strategies can be effective and are often necessary in struggles for specific kinds of material or political goals—such as access to economic resources or political and cultural representation—they ultimately cannot allow for the kinds of transformation of self and world that are necessary for a lasting manifestation of justice and equality. Such strategies are always locked in a position of reclaiming power from the sources that produced a sense of powerlessness in the first place. Audre Lorde's words, "the master's tools can never be used to dismantle the master's house,"[13] have been exhaustively cited by feminist activists and intellectuals concerned with such questions. This phrase has often been interpreted by students whom I have taught as a separatist or revolutionary call which entails a complete dissociation from the "master"—the particular oppressor in question (for instance white, male, rich). The system, it is assumed in this interpretation, can never be changed from reform within. Yet the powerful challenge that Lorde's words present is much more far-reaching than even such a distinction between reformism and revolution. For with the rich histories of activism and the vast intellectual discourses on social justice we have to draw on, at this moment in history we still for the most part implicitly frame our words and actions on the foundations of the master's house—either by making claims for access to this house or by trying to construct houses of our own. The heart of the assumption that we often operate with is that the shelter, security and ownership of the master's house is in fact in the master's hands. It is this assumption that has led to a situation where the alternative "houses" which intellectuals and activists have built—organizations, fields of knowledge, projects for social justice, resistance movements—have often replicated or produced the structures of power that they set out to combat. The result is the foreclosure of a vision of social justice which can rest on a radical form of disidentification, a letting go of all forms and elements of what we perceive as constituting our identity while being fully engaged in confronting the very real inequalities and exclusions which existing constructions of identity do produce. It is this possibility of disidentification that can provide an important foundation for action for those who are committed to addressing questions of inequality and justice.

As a teacher, I have often struggled with helping students maintain enough detachment to confront the sense of implication and defensiveness that they feel when they realize that they are implicated in structures of privilege. In one instance, in order to try and overcome such stumbling blocks in the class' discussion of the larger issues at hand, I turned to the class and asked them to let go of all of the larger concepts and questions and theories and problems which they had been struggling to grasp all semester and to simply think of their own selves. Turning to them I then asked, "If you let go of all of these structures and aspects of identity and location which supposedly define you—of family, race, gender, sexuality, class and nationality—what would be left? How would you then define your 'self'?" The question left the class of twenty graduate students in silence. In a remarkable moment it became clear that the students did not have the language to think about or talk about themselves, or of feminism, in ways that did not rest on some notion of identity. This was not because of some intrinsic shortcoming of the students, but because of the limits of the languages of politics and justice they had access to.

Despite all of the so-called fluidity of the boundaries of identity and the crossing of borders in this so-called postmodern globalized world, the class could not find the words to publicly speak of a sense of self which did not rest on some external form of identification. It was a question that we left unanswered and one which we never formally returned to in class discussion. It is at this pregnant moment of silence that I believe that many of the practices and theories of movements such as the feminist movement have stumbled; and it is precisely at this edgy pool of silence that I want to begin to think about the possibility of a disidentified self that can lead us to a different set of political practices engaged with questions of inequality and justice.

THE PRACTICE OF DISIDENTIFICATION

What does it mean to simultaneously espouse an unrelenting confrontation of all privileges and exclusions based on identity while espousing a political practice based on disidentification? Disidentification is not a "new" fashionable theoretical concept, the latest in the line of intellectual commodities for the knowledge market.[14] The movement to a state of disidentification is a long and arduous journey, one that involves an unceasing stripping away of all of what may seem like unending layers of attachment to various forms of power, privilege, security and self-interest. The most self-evident of these layers are of course those that we have come to view as a familiar list of social identities—of race, nation, class, ethnicity, sexuality, caste, gender and religion. Disidentifying from such identities requires a dual process. At one level, it necessitates confronting the real effects of such identities, including the personal privileges one may gain from them. At a second level, it requires being able to detach one's own self-definition from such externally- and self-imposed identities. This may sound like a contradictory process but it is, I believe, the only way in which real questions of power, privilege, identity and difference can be simultaneously confronted and transcended.

Consider how this might unfold in relation to classroom situations. As I have noted, a central challenge in teaching about social movements such as feminism is to enable to students to confront both the privilege and marginalization which their social identities and locations bring to their personal lives and communities without turning such a confrontation into guilt, resistance or a defensive claim to authenticity. It is here that a politics of disidentification is of fundamental importance in navigating such questions in a healthy and constructive manner. Students must *dis*identify from their own privilege in order to clearly analyze and, indeed, take responsibility for how that privilege shapes the most intimate aspects of their lives. Students who are initially exposed to such issues of difference and privilege often do not have the psychic space to understand that they do not need to identify with the various labels which are placed on them (and which they may claim for themselves) while simultaneously recognizing that these identity-based labels are *real* and that they do confer real *material* privileges onto groups and individuals. For instance a strategy for white students dealing with racial privilege would be to recognize and address the social and economic forms of power and privilege associated with whiteness in contemporary society in the United States while realizing that their own conceptions of their self do not need to rest on such hegemonic conceptions of "whiteness."

Or consider another situation which has arisen in the aftermath of the 9/11 attacks in the U.S. The mainstream media has endlessly posed and debated the question: "Why do they hate us?" (where "they" usually refers to a generalized and confused sense of Muslims or Arabs or in some cases general "Third World" civilian populations who are critical of the U.S.). In framing the question in this way, the mainstream U.S. media and politicians are able to collapse the distinction between criticisms of U.S. foreign policy and a sentiment of personal hatred against Americans. While many Americans have been misled by this confusion, individuals and social groups who have understood and worked to change the negative effects of many of the U.S. government's policies are able to disidentify from this hegemonic sense of American identity being imposed on them. Seen in this way, it should be clear that disidentification is not an abstraction but a practical process.

The difficult nature of disidentification is that it is not limited to a single identity such as one's national identity. Disidentifying from nationalism provides a clear example because individuals committed to social justice, and feminism in particular, have usually undergone such a process through their activism and writing. However, the process becomes more difficult when it relates to other social identities (such as gender or race) which may be experienced in a more personal sense. Yet it is precisely such difficulty that represents the heart of disidentification—it is a process which operates from a place of risk rather than from a place of safety.[15] Disidentification in effect demands the very opposite of the safe space that has often been sought by feminists. It requires a journey where we must be willing to confront the deepest sources of our own complicity in the external structures of power we want to change. And in this journey, it requires a willingness to let go of the false images we might have of ourselves without reverting back to the safe-houses of identity which attempt to keep out those who disrupt these images. It is this sense of risk which a politics of disidentification has the courage to embrace.

I have so far been speaking of disidentification in relation to more conventional senses of social identity in part because such identities are easier to grasp and are often visible issues for social justice movements. However, the practice of disidentification is a much deeper process that also requires a letting go of more subtle forms of attachment beyond these identities. For example, for writers and activists it may involve letting go of rigid attachments to ideologies in order to learn from emerging ideas of new movements and from different (both younger and older) generations. So many of the splits in left movements have stemmed from leaders and activists being unable to let go of their attachments to their own visions of what is the true or right ideology (consider, for instance, the resistance of many leftist movements to taking gender to be as serious a social inequality as class or race). This begins to take us to a more subtle understanding of disidentification as a process of letting go not just of external social identities but of various forms of often invisible ego-based attachments such as public recognition or a sense of intellectual or ideological superiority. The process is difficult because it necessitates a move away from romanticized self-images that we may hold as writers or activists committed to social justice to a more painful and honest confrontation with our own investments in and attachments to power. While the precise nature of such a journey will vary with the circumstances of the individual what should be clear is that this is a practical process that ultimately must be lived rather than debated.

Yet the question that remains is: What does this journey lead to? What would the answer be to the question I posed to my class: "If you let go of all of these structures and aspects of identity and location which supposedly define you—of family, race, gender, sexuality, class and nationality—what would be left?" Postmodern theorists who have engaged in the task of taking apart the idea of identity (showing how it is constructed, imposed and fluid) have usually stopped short of providing an answer. The result is that in the academy, students are usually given important tools with which to take apart—to deconstruct—such ideas but no vision of an alternative form of self to work towards. While there is much to be learned from strategies of deconstruction, social transformation demands the risk of providing an alternative. In other words, if a politics of disidentification is to serve as a basis for transformation, it cannot just be a negative process of moving away from identity. It must also be a process of moving towards this alternative disidentified self.

THE POSSIBILITIES OF THE DISIDENTIFIED SELF

What then would the discussion of the question that I posed to the class have looked like? To begin, I suggest that we must confront the question of spirituality—a confrontation which both modern and postmodern scholars, as well as activists committed to progressive social and political transformation, have usually tended not to engage with in an explicit manner. Even postmodern definitions of the self have been bounded in very subtle and implicit ways—bounded by the contexts of history, culture, social location and sometimes simply by a kind of instrumental assumption that we can simply fashion ourselves by deploying our identities in strategic and fluid ways. And, for all of the vast richness of feminist theory and the often aching attention to specificities of cultural context and difference, there has been a remarkable absence of even the possibility of a divinized conception of the self—the self as spirit.[16] One of the saddest moments which I can remember in over ten years of teaching is when I was talking with a group of Women's Studies students and one of the students "confessed" that she had a real interest in questions of feminism and spirituality but was afraid to talk about them because she felt people associated these issues with the kind of stuff Oprah Winfrey did on her afternoon talk shows.[17]

I suggest that it is only an understanding of the self as spirit, as well as matter and mind, and an understanding of the spiritual as a real force that permeates everything we are and everything we do that can provide us with the foundation for the kind of disidentified self which is necessary to realize our visions of social transformation. It is an understanding that there is an essence of self that transcends differences and divisions. However, this essence of the self is not the same as reverting back to an essentialized identity. Feminists have rightly pointed to the problems of gender essentialism—that is, the assumption that women and men are reducible to fixed, homogeneous identities (for example, women as essentially nurturing or weak and men as essentially aggressive, violent, dominant). Such criticisms have also argued against the false assumption that women share an essential gender identity not shaped by differences such class, race, sexuality or nation. The idea of a spiritual essence is the very antithesis of such an essentialism of identity, since spirit can never be contained within the limits of identity.[18] It is this unboundedness of the disidentified self which feminist theorist Trinh Minh-ha is hinting at when she speaks of the "infinite layers" of the self.[19] It is a sense of the self which contains within it a radical interconnection between all of us that necessarily transcends narrower forms of identification. Jacqui Alexander points to this universal relationship when she speaks of a "deep knowing that we are in fact interdependent, neither separate nor autonomous. As human beings, we have a sacred connection to one another, and this is why enforced separations wreak havoc on our souls."[20] Universalism here does not imply sameness (the old assumption that "we are all the same so difference doesn't matter") but rather speaks to the interconnection that exists within the self: the possibility of recognizing that the world exists within each of us. The difference between this and older forms of universalism and essentialism is that the practice of disidentification acknowledges that this universal self is simultaneously present within the very real social identities, differences and inequalities which shape our locations, attitudes and visions of our lives and worlds. Speaking of a spiritual self does not dislodge the materiality of these identities; rather, it requires a full and complete confrontation with the various sources of power, privilege and oppression which shape our lives so that this spiritual self can emerge.[21]

The spiritualized nature of the process of disidentification is crucial in taking us beyond conventional discussions of power, privilege and identity. Such discussions have traditionally been based on a presumption of a bounded material realm—whether defined in more conventional terms of access to and ownership of resources or in terms of the materiality of discourse (the power-laden meanings, languages and forms of knowledge that shape our lives). However, the process of disidentification which I am speaking of must also be a fundamentally spiritual process if it is to effectively dismantle the vast structures of power which shape our lives. Spirituality can serve as a tremendous source of power that can enable us to challenge some of our deepest practices of identification, and can lead us to understand our self as an infinite, unbounded source of divinity, spiritual strength and empowerment. It leads us to question our ingrained assumptions regarding the boundaries of individual autonomy, agency and rationality. It leads us to question the often hidden distinctions we make between mind, matter and spirit. It dares us to disrupt the careful lines which thinkers and activists, both modern and postmodern, both religious and secular, have carved out between the realms of the human and divine.

THE PRACTICE OF THE DISIDENTIFIED SELF

What does this divinized understanding of the self mean in real, practical terms for the difficult struggles for social, political and economic equality in this world? A practical disidentified self? How and in what way? Too often a spiritualized understanding of the self is used as a basis for transcendent, otherworldly spiritual and religious practices. The assumption made is that one can turn away from or cope with, for example, extreme poverty or inequality because this world is just a temporary waiting room, so to speak, which enlightened individuals must seek to escape. A disidentified body would in this view simply cease to identify with the concerns of this world. Wars, after all, have been fought throughout history. Poverty has always existed. Empires have risen and fallen. This kind of escapism, though it is sometimes mistaken for spirituality, is not what I mean.

In the deepest sense in which I understand it, the disidentified activist simultaneously engages in both a radical movement for complete social, economic and political justice and in a profound spiritual journey. The simultaneity of this process lies in the simple fact that from the eye of the disidentified subject there is no possible separation between spirituality and social justice. The presumed separation in fact is only an illusory boundary which has been produced by the edifices of power of various religious political, economic and social establishments. Furthermore, I suggest that it is only a politics based on disidentification that can result in the kind of lasting transformation that individuals and groups committed to social justice have struggled for so long to manifest. Indeed, from the eye of the disidentified subject, this form of transformation is not a game of an inventive imagination but a realizable possibility.

It is not a question of simply sitting back and assuming that acknowledging our spiritual selves will automatically lead us to a transformative space. Nor is it simply a return to an easy universalism which smugly says "identity doesn't matter" in order to evade confronting material structures of privilege. It is a process that, by necessity, challenges our deepest ego-driven identifications which shape our aspirations for recognition, success, superiority. Of all of the forms of inequality and domination which I have been reflecting on, it is these personal attachments to power which can be the most difficult to transform. Yet without such transformation it would be impossible for a social justice, activist or intellectual movement to be effective in the long run. For without this disidentification, even the most laudable goals can become entangled in ego investments and in both individual and group interests in control, leadership and self-image. It is here that progressive activists and intellectuals can benefit from one of the simplest and most powerful teachings that has permeated most spiritual traditions—the need to engage in an honest and continual process of self-examination and self-transformation.

Traditional political movements and their ideologies have limited this simple truth through the frames of identity and consciousness—focusing, for instance, on the need to raise our consciousness of broader social inequalities and internalized forms of power and oppression that we carry around with us. While such approaches are necessary for any broader process of social transformation, they are not sufficient. What I am suggesting is that external social transformation cannot occur if it does not simultaneously engage in a complete process of self-transformation, one that transforms even the most subtle forms of attachment to power and self-aggrandizement. Such forms of attachments are very subtle, yet particularly powerful, amongst those who claim to speak or act for the good of "the oppressed." For those who teach, it is easiest to recognize such dynamics in the classroom. I have, for instance, lost count of the number of times when students who have come to understand broader structures of inequality and who are usually motivated by an absolutely sincere passion for justice, physically contort their faces or speak with an assumed air of superiority when their classmates voice what are perceived as "unenlightened" opinions on social justice. In contemporary American public culture this has been mistakenly tagged as a problem with political correctness, the implication being that the problem is with the political attitudes of individuals or groups who adamantly focus on questions of injustice and discrimination.

The problem is not, however, political in a narrow sense of political intolerance. Rather, I suggest it is a spiritual problem that has tremendous political effects. But why call this a spiritual problem rather than simply a problem with difficult or immature personalities? It is a spiritual problem, I have come to believe, because all such ego-driven investments arise out of a misconception of a bounded, identity-driven self and out of a lack of self-knowledge that stems from this misconception. Individuals who act and write out of the deepest understanding and passion for justice are often faced with severe external obstacles and contexts that are unsympathetic, if not hostile, to transformative politics of any kind. In the face of such external difficulties, it is easy to begin to view one's own knowledge and commitment as a superior good intrinsic to one's own personality. The result is a process of identification where knowledge and justice become associated with one's bounded self-conceptions. And of course, as is often the case, such identifications then easily merge with material interests—the control of organizations and agendas, positions of leadership, career prospects, success, fame, status.

Consider the way in which an alternative approach based on a spiritualized understanding of the self can enable practical work for social justice through an example of a grassroots women's organization in Suriname which Gloria Wekker has analyzed.[22] Wekker describes the ways in which Afro-Surinamese cultural and spiritual traditions contain an understanding of selfhood which disrupts traditional Western ideas of the self as a bounded, rational individual. She describes the Afro-Surinamese concept of "odo" (proverb/oral culture) which "suggests that the subject is made up of various 'instances,' including gods and the spirits of ancestors, and that all of these need to be acknowledged and held in harmony" (331). This understanding of the self, which defies any separation between the material and spiritual self, or between the individual and transcendent dimensions of selfhood, is inextricably linked to the emergence of the organization Mofina Brasa. This organization is committed to serving the economic, political and cultural needs of poor women, yet such "material" concerns are inseparable from the Afro-Suriname spiritual traditions in which "human beings are understood to be partly biological and partly spiritual beings" (335). As Wekker notes, when she asked Renate Druiventak, the founder of the group, about the origin of the organization's name, Druiventak told her "it had been whispered to her by her *winti* (spirits/gods) in a dream" (345). Consider the ways in which such a perspective radically transforms existing approaches to identity-based, individualized views of leadership: it represents a radical break from the market-driven model of competition of leadership that often underlies even feminist organizations as individuals compete with one another for recognition as the sole leaders, founders or producers of original ideas and activities.

I believe what is at stake here are two simple truths. First, that all sources of power and understanding that we find within us stem from a spiritual or universal source, and that these sources are equally present and equally accessible in all individuals—regardless of their political ideologies, material standing, social identities or religious claims and disclaimers. Second, that any kind of transformative politics, if it is to be effective, must start from an understanding that all of us, each and every single individual without exception, no matter how politically or spiritually enlightened we believe we are, contain within us and enact the ego-driven investments of power and identification which I have been speaking of. It is only from this point of honest, humble, if sometimes uncomfortable, self-recognition that the kind of spiritual, political, social and economic global transformation which social activists seek can unfold, a transformation which is not a luxury, fantasy or desire, but a necessity for global survival. This is what a politics based on disidentification has come to mean to me—a politics that is neither easy nor inevitable in our struggles for social justice.

Such possibilities for a practical form of radical disidentification have already been embodied in the writings and lives of individual feminists of color. Consider for instance the process of disidentification which feminist thinker and activist Gloria Anzaldúa depicts in her well-known book, *Borderlands/La Frontera: The New Mestiza. Borderlands* is a classic text in Women's Studies courses and many feminist writers have used Anzaldúa's analysis of the borderlands, the psychological and physical border culture between the U.S. and Mexico to examine the complexities of identity formation for individuals and groups who occupy liminal spaces in society. Yet while Anzaldúa's work has been used variously as a representative text of Latina women,[23] women of color and Third World women, the depth of Anzaldúa's critical vision has often been lost in this identity-based deployment of her text. In fact, Anzaldúa's work represents a remarkable political, historical and biographical representation which disrupts all oppositions between the material and spiritual worlds.[24] As she puts it,

We're not supposed to remember such otherworldly events. We're supposed to ignore, forget, kill those fleeting images of the soul's presence and of the spirit's presence. We've been taught that the spirit is outside our bodies or above our heads somewhere up in the sky with God. We're supposed to forget that every cell in our bodies, every bone and every bird and worm has spirit in it. (36)

Yet for Anzaldúa the spiritual transformation of self cannot be disconnected from what are normally classified as the "real" material structures of oppression that have shaped her life and history as a queer Chicana feminist in the United States. Her political-biographical-psychic representation is one of incredible depths of pain, as she breaks out and contests dualistic constructions of the spiritual and material. Spirituality, in Anzaldúa's vision and experience, is not an easy escape from the agony of the material world. Such a dualistic opposition does not exist in her understanding. For Anzaldúa, the external structures of oppression such as race, class and gender are fundamentally linked to the cage of rationality, what she calls "the 'official' reality of the rational, reasoning mode" (36), which blocks off any notion of a spiritual understanding of the world, what she calls "la facultad." In fact, the very experience of exclusion and oppression can provide an opening to this form of understanding, this "capacity to see in surface phenomena the meaning of deeper realities" (38). It is often a painful break from the comforts of material security and the various attachments of our everyday lives—family, community, country—which provides for an opening up to this understanding of reality. She writes, "As we plunge vertically, the break, with its accompanying new seeing, makes us pay attention to the soul, and we are thus carried into awareness—an experiencing of soul (Self)" (39). Yet there is nothing easy or inevitable in this process of self-transformation. On the contrary, Anzaldúa represents her transformation as a process of being "devoured" by *Coatlique*, the serpent goddess, that she invokes from her cultural-spiritual mesoamerican history. This is not the sanitized, circumscribed, patriarchal or "feminist" celebration of goddess power which has been appropriated in hegemonic forms in recent times; Anzaldúa's spiritual process has nothing to do with the easy externalized form of goddess worship that is sometimes mistaken as a feminist reclaiming of spirituality.[25] If anything, Anzaldúa depicts *Coatlique* as a state of darkness and "crisis," "the consuming internal whirlwind" (46) out of which growth and learning is possible but not inevitable. "The *Coatlique* state," as she puts it, "can be a way station or it can be a way of life (46)—the direction depends on the choices and labor which each individual is prepared to put into this kind of revolutionary transformation of the self.

Anzaldúa's *Borderlands* is a vivid example of the kinds of processes which must unfold in the manifestation of a politics of disidentification. A broader transformation of external structures of power can never fully occur if we do not simultaneously transform the internal investments of power that exist within ourselves. Too often, in the context of contemporary feminism, this confrontation of self has been translated into a list of social inequalities and identities which must be addressed—race, class, gender, sexuality, etc. Judith Butler has called attention to what she terms "an embarrassed 'etc.'" which often concludes this list and has suggested that this "etc." marks the limitation of dealing with named, identity-based politics.[26] The "etc." in fact bursts with significance precisely because the kind of transformation of self that we must have the courage to embrace cannot be contained within a finite list of external social identities. Yet while postmodern critics have often insightfully pointed to the limitations of identity-based politics,[27] they have usually not understood the deeper significance of this necessary withering away of identity. Too often, in postmodern understandings, disidentification has been recast as a celebration of a directionless form of indeterminacy or a denial of the very real material effects of identities which structure the lives of individuals and social groups in very rigid ways. The stumbling block for postmodern thinkers has been that while they have provided us with useful insights into the limits of dualistic thinking, the paired oppositions that are at the basis of existing structures of power that have often hindered our visions of justice (man/woman, black/white, identity/difference), they have not broken into the realm of consciousness which Anzaldúa calls "la facultad." It is for this reason that traditional postmodern scholars often must remain at the level of interrogating discourses and relations of power without being able to connect this form of interrogation to a viable alternative of transformation.

Interrogations of power-laden categories such as identity, in this context, simply become a way of life, an end in themselves, rather than a way station to a deeper transformative politics of disidentification.

What I am suggesting, then, is that if our politics and movements are to be able to fully challenge existing structures of power and inequality they must also rest on a form of spiritual transformation. Such a transformation requires a complete dissociation from the ego-based investments in control, recognition and superiority which are mistakenly identified as self-interest. It requires a brutally honest, inward process of self-examination to dispel the idealized self-images we carry around with us and provide the kind of radical humility required to really manifest social justice in this world. It requires that we confront the fears and resistances to the existence of the unknowable and the transcendent, both within us and within this world. And it requires a firm understanding that there can be no separation between this internal process of confrontation and what we view as external processes of change and transformation.

This is of course not a quick recipe for social activism. But if we face for a moment the vastness of the structures of oppression which imprison this world, why would any of us believe for a moment that any movement for social justice and transformation would be easy? This is a question I have often posed to students whom I have taught as they have become overwhelmed by the enormity of what they must learn about the world and the immensity of the connections and inequalities which permeate our lives. In many ways, what I have been arguing here is more overwhelming than even an acknowledgment of such external inequalities because what I am saying is that the hidden, seemingly benign jealousies, fears, desires and ambitions which all of us, without exception, harbor within are actually not hidden and not benign. These internal feelings are simply smaller versions of the larger structures of power that we care about; simply being committed to social justice in its external form does not lessen the significance of our internal ego investments — on the contrary, it makes these investments more significant. For one of the basic spiritual teachings across many traditions which feminism has sometimes lost is that it is usually easier to identify and condemn the errors which others commit than it is to face our own.

Yet there is also reason to be more hopeful, because in an era where the vastness of material structures of inequality are so overwhelming and where progressive movements for social justice, rather than making progress, are more often than not struggling to prevent further onslaughts of repression, a spiritualized vision provides a perspective of hope and possibility. Even a moment of disidentification from the claims we are so caught up making in our lives dispels the myths of control which privileged individuals, groups and nations hold onto. Disidentified from such structures, both internal and external, transformation is no longer an unrealizable utopia, nor is it a limited battle based on retribution and oppositional politics. The disidentified self does not sit in opposition against anyone, even in the midst of immense political struggle and contestation. For one of the simplest understandings which movements such as feminism can benefit from is that, from a spiritualized perspective, what are viewed as utopian visions of absolute equality and justice are realizable. We only forget when we identify with the structures of power we are trying to unravel.

In teaching about feminism and Women's Studies in the United States, I have found that one of the biggest sources of confusion for students is the relationship between theory and practice. Most students come to the study of women and feminism with varying combinations of a desire for self-liberation and a desire to change the lives of other women. What they find, however, is a complicated set of debates which implicate privileged women in wider social inequalities of nation, race and class. These debates, sparked by the activist and academic writings over the past two decades by women of the color in the U.S. and feminists from "Third World" countries,[1] have pointed to the ways in which feminists in the United States who have focused exclusively on fighting against gender inequality have often reproduced hierarchies such as race, class and sexuality.[2] Meanwhile feminists who have focused on international issues, particularly in Third World countries, have questioned the ways in which activism based on the belief in a global form of sisterhood has failed to address long histories of colonialism as well as more recent relationships of power between the United States and countries in the Third World. As feminists began to call attention to the ways in which privileged groups of women themselves are implicated in and often benefit materially from various structures of power, they began to shake beliefs in a romanticized form of global sisterhood and in the presumed innocence of feminist activism.[3] Feminist activists have also attempted to address such issues, resulting in, for instance, movements for global feminist alliances that draw on recent insights by feminists of color about the intersections between race, class and gender in conceptualizing women's rights.[4]

A particular complication in current discussions of feminist activism has to do with the ways in which governments and nationalist forces have used women and the language of women's rights to serve their own ideological purposes. The most recent visible instance of this in the United States has, of course, been the ways in which the brutal repression of Afghan women under the Taliban regime became a form of moral justification for the bombing of Afghanistan in the first phase of America's "war on terrorism."[5] Examples of this type reappear throughout history. The need to protect women has long been used as justification for military action to defend the sovereignty of communities, nations and civilizations. For example, in the eighteenth and nineteenth centuries, European powers developed ideologies regarding the oppression of women to justify their colonization of Asia, Africa and the Middle East, focusing on cultural forms of oppression such as widow burning in India and veiling in the Middle East to provide fuel for a morally superior form of Western civilizing project.[6] In other words, the oppression of women in colonized areas was used to defend European rule as a superior form of rule over "native" men who were portrayed as being too uncivilized to govern themselves. The power of these colonial histories is still evident today, as images of oppressed Third World women, particularly of veiled women, continue to serve as an ideological justification for the current U.S. war on terrorism.

In response to these forms of colonial ideologies, nationalist movements and governments in the Third World, both secular and religious, have often too easily adopted defenses that have also used women as symbolic tools for their own agendas. By asserting a fixed cultural difference from "the West," these nation-states have sought to excuse or conceal deep gendered structures of inequality.[7] For instance, governments and conservative political movements in non-Western nations will often brand women's organizations and struggles for women's rights as "Westernized" movements in order to delegitimize their demands for equality and justice.

In the context of a rapidly globalizing world where ideologies and images travel quickly through the media, it has become increasingly difficult to separate out such cross-cutting agendas and ideologies from local, practical concerns with women's rights. Such dynamics have complicated the question of feminist activism in the United States, particularly because U.S. feminism has a stronger focus on the cultural oppression of non-Western women than on the links between women's oppression and colonialism, U.S. foreign policy and vast international economic disparities.[8] Feminists and women's organizations, usually struggling with scant resources and immense political and social obstacles, continually risk being implicated in the kinds of power relationships that reproduce the very structures of inequality which constrain the lives of women they are trying to aid. This dynamic is overtly manifested in the United States, where dominant economic and military power invests the languages, activities and agendas of even progressive movements such as the women's movement with forms of power and control that are simply not present in other parts of the world. For example, U.S.-based feminists have the power to frame, in significant ways, agendas and debates for international conferences because of their greater access to economic resources and because of the ways in which intellectual debates in the U.S. continue to shape the terms of debates in other countries.[9]

THE FEMINIST DILEMMA OF THEORY AND PRACTICE

Confrontations with the power relations that connect women's lives have contributed in substantial ways to debates in feminist theory. Feminist theorists, for instance, have questioned the implications of using the category of "woman" as a basis for political action; they have argued that "woman" has often stood for heterosexual, middle-class, white women.[10] This has led to a great deal of confusion in the discussion of theory and practice. On the one hand, the complexity of intersecting structures of inequality both locally and globally has led some to resist such insights and claim that the focus on "difference" is an abstract theoretical exercise and an obstacle to unified women's activism. On the other hand, feminist theorists who do criticize the exclusionary tendencies of mainstream feminism have often left students and readers at this point of criticism without elaborating on the ways in which such criticisms can lead to new or different forms of transformative action that do not reproduce exclusions and that do not get caught in the ideological manipulations of governments and nationalist movements.

The result has been that the definition of practice in most feminist debates has largely remained within a fairly conventional framework of meaning. "Practice" is usually understood in two central ways. First, it is defined through a kind of negative definition, as action that is not located in the academy. Second, practice is viewed in the conventional terms of struggling for women's rights, for equality between men and women, and for access to various kinds of resources—whether economic, political, institutional or cultural. Debates on the links between theory and practice have then centered on the question of how to translate academic and theoretical analyses of women's lives into practice, that is, into acts relevant to women outside of the academy. While the intent to move beyond the confines of elite American academic institutions and to work to better the lives of less-privileged women is an undeniably necessary one, this debate on theory and practice has ultimately foreclosed a deeper understanding and critical transformation of the meaning of practice.

This foreclosure has been most vividly evident to me as a teacher. When students challenge the point of analyzing all of the complexities that shape women's lives they commonly do so on the grounds that feminist knowledge and theory is irrelevant for real activism and practice. In many instances, this is channeled into a wider resistance to inaccessible and difficult language associated with new forms of theory, usually assumed to be "postmodern" theory.[11] Yet I have found that these instances of resistance actually have less to do with the accessibility of academic writing style than they do with an acute paralysis that these students feel when faced with the overwhelming structures of power in which they are themselves implicated. Students are frustrated not by the difficulty of abstract, theoretical or "academic" language but by the fact that they are not given the tools to think about alternative forms of practice that do not repeat exclusions of the past or help them move past their privileges in the present. This was starkly apparent to me during the course of one graduate class that I taught on contemporary feminism. Many students reacted against the texts which sought to examine hierarchies of race, class and nation that exist between women in various contexts and were mostly written by women of color in the U.S. and internationally. They claimed that the texts were too complicated and not relevant to real life.[12] Yet the class was most interested in the session where we read a small selection from the postmodern theorist Michel Foucault. At the end of the semester, when I asked students for suggestions on what readings they would like to see more of, they all indicated they wanted to read more Foucault. Clearly, the resistance of the students was not to theory but to texts which challenged them to confront hierarchies and histories of race and colonialism that shape the lives of women, of feminist thought and of practice itself. The students in the class wanted to learn new and complex forms of theory but when it came to discussions of feminism and activism they wanted to revert back to versions that did not deal with power relations between women; the meaning, definitions and effects of feminist practice would thus be left unexamined and kept safe from the critical realm of theory.

The problem in this theory-practice split is twofold. Students have been shortchanged both by "deconstructive" feminist theories (that simply deconstruct or take apart the problems with existing forms of feminism without offering alternative practices that can lead to social transformation) and by the narrow and unexamined boundaries that define what counts as feminist practice. I have a vivid memory of one Women's Studies graduate course on feminist theory which I taught. A large section of the students had been discontented from the very beginning of the semester since they were registered for an M.A. degree and were interested in questions of practice rather than theory; as they indicated, they were intent on becoming activists not academics. After a few weeks of struggling to get them to read and discuss the assigned materials, I suggested that we simply put aside the readings for the day and spend some time talking about feminist practice. I asked them to tell me what they meant by practice and to discuss what kinds of things they wanted to do outside the academy so that we could find ways to connect the course to their own specific, activist-oriented interests. The question was met with dead silence. What became clear from the silence was that the students in fact were not sure what they meant by practice. They had a general sense of wanting to work for social change but were unsure of how that translated into practical action. At the most, I have found that such students end up with definitions of practice as participation in formal non-governmental organizations (NGOs) or other community-based or political organizations. The point is not that such organizations do not engage in important and necessary programs for the social and economic improvement of women (and men) but rather, that there is a lack of focus on the dailiness of practice—both at an individual level as well as in terms of the *dailiness* of practices which organizations engage in. A narrow definition of practice prevents students from seeing that criticisms of the exclusionary nature of some models of feminism are not a theoretical stumbling block but a sign that calls us to pay more attention to the dailiness of practice, for instance by addressing the everyday ways in which one's racial, national or class identity may inadvertently produce exclusions and hierarchies.

One of feminism's primary projects has been to question distinctions between the public and private and to expose how this separation has served to devalue and constrain women's work and social roles. Yet it is this very distinction that now forms the unspoken, commonsense definition of feminist practice. Practice, in this model, represents participation in public, formal organizational activity aimed at improving women's lives. Yet it is precisely the question of what counts as practice that must be radically contested and opened up if there is any real hope of realizing the kind of broad social transformation that both academics and activists who are committed to feminism and to questions of social justice strive for. Thus, rather than remaining paralyzed by the theory/practice dilemma of feminism, I want to suggest ways in which the problems that have surfaced in this debate can lead us to rethink our definitions of practice.

There is a need for an expanded understanding of feminist practice that links existing forms of social activism with notions of ethical action as well as with a spiritualized practice and philosophy of non-violence. This approach can provide the building blocks for a form of feminist practice that transcends the pitfalls that currently limit the transformative potential of feminism. For instance, everyday ethical action is a necessary element for any form of practice to be transformative. For, from a spiritualized perspective, a form of activism that espouses noble public principles and actions but rests on everyday practices that draw on even subtle ego-based hierarchy, exclusion or competition cannot be transformative because they are acts that injure the spirit. At another level, movements for social justice that rest on strategies of retribution that are violent either in physical, material[13] or spiritual terms also limit the possibilities of a deeper lasting form of transformation because they ultimately mirror the kinds of structures of oppression they seek to overturn. A spiritualized practice of non-violence can provide the elements for the development of a form of transformative feminist practice that can transcend the limitations inherent in older models of activism that have reproduced hierarchies and exclusions. Such a form of practice moves beyond distinctions between the dailiness of practice and organized social activism. Furthermore, it can permanently dislodge the paralysis produced by purely deconstructive forms of theories, move beyond the polarized theory/practice divide and demonstrate the ways in which real social transformation is possible.

THE MEANING OF ETHICAL PRACTICE

What then would the building blocks of this kind of transformative practice look like? The first step in finding an answer lies in the development of a form of practice that integrates feminism's existing focus on social and economic inequalities in the material world with a deeper sense of ethical and spiritual practice. The Dalai Lama has posited a useful distinction between the ethical and spiritual components of practice. He has described spirituality in relation to "qualities of the human spirit—such as love and compassion, patience, tolerance, forgiveness, contentment, a sense of responsibility, a sense of harmony" (22), qualities which he goes on to note are "defined by an implicit concern for others' well-being" (23). Ethical action, meanwhile, is defined in relation to a principle concerned with avoiding acts of harm and injury against others.[14] This distinction provides a useful starting point for a discussion of feminist practice. A practice of non-violent transformation must include both the ethical and the spiritual. The ethical component represents a first step in this process, and ultimately becomes a part of a larger, spiritualized form of transformative feminist practice.

Ethical concerns are often the foundation for the kind of public and service-oriented activism that feminism has taken up. However, if the deeper ethical principles that underlie such activities are not an explicit component of these practices, it is more likely than not that organizational hierarchies or other forms of power will eventually permeate and curtail the real transformative potential of such activism, regardless of whether it continues to produce material benefits for the constituencies being targeted. I have found in discussions with students that this subtle process of corruption has often been mistakenly confused with a debate on the pros and cons of working within "the system," that is, within formal institutions such as academic or governmental settings. What I am suggesting is that the potential for the corruption of ethics is as prevalent within social movements or activist political organizations as it is within "the system." Feminists need to guard against isolating questions of tactics and methods of action in their practice (for example, what kind of organization to build or what strategies to use) from its ethical and spiritual components.

At one level, a concern with ethical questions would seem to be a self-evident part of feminism. For instance, from a feminist perspective it is clear that patriarchal ideologies and practices that cause harm to women by seeking to limit and control women's lives, bodies and sexualities would constitute a form of unethical practice. Feminism thus has an ethical dimension present in its agenda. However, the question I want to focus on is not one of simply recognizing that the goals and visions of feminism contains within them a significant ethical component (whether that component is made explicit or not). Rather, it is a question of what it means to translate this ethical component into an integral part of feminist practice. Too often, feminists have assumed that since the goal of working for women's rights, liberation and freedom (whatever the framework may be) is an ethical or politically noble goal, then the acts of those committed to such goals are automatically ethical acts. This usually leads to the view that abstract discussions of ethics are best left to the theorists while activists must engage in the real business of effecting social change. There is an implied division between theory (defined as critical or "philosophical" discussions of ethics) and practice (defined as engaging in political activism for a particular cause). The hidden assumption is that activism and the struggle for social change is an intrinsically ethical practice. In fact, however, it is not.

This is, I will admit, a controversial charge, and one which I will try to explain further. For any form of social activism or feminist practice to represent a form of ethical practice it must begin by linking the dailiness of an individual's behavior with her or his more public, formal activity that is engaged in service of others. Of course it seems much nobler to speak of broader social transformation and to engage in acts designed to save others from very real forms of economic and social oppression. Yet how are we to challenge social inequalities in the world "out there" if we reproduce these exclusions and hierarchies in our own everyday practices? These kinds of paradoxes have been at the heart of some of the conflicts regarding difference within the feminist movement, for example when feminists of color have criticized the exclusionary nature of mainstream feminism. This is an overt example of the question of ethical contradictions I am pointing to. However, such contradictions also take more subtle forms which are not reducible to structural forms of prejudice based on identities such as race, class or sexuality. For instance, in both academic and activist organizations individuals often act in ways that may cause personal injury to others in more subtle everyday acts — for instance through gossip, slander, and competitiveness. While these may seem like small ethical errors compared to more obvious forms of social exclusion, they in fact mirror the same forms of power that underpin social inequalities based on race, sexuality or class, for they violate an understanding of the interconnectedness between all individuals that is crucial for any lasting form of social transformation.

To view these kinds of acts and attitudes as private "personal" qualities is to perpetuate the worst kind of dichotomy between the public and private which feminism has sought for so long to contest. For a long time in the United States, one of the most well-known feminist slogans has been "the personal is political." Yet surprisingly this slogan has for the most part not been understood in terms of its deepest ethical implications. To view the notion of the personal as political as meaning that "private" issues such as domestic violence, gendered hierarchies within the family or reproductive rights are political issues that must be struggled for is important, but it is only half of the picture. The other half is that if, as feminism has rightly argued, the personal is the political, then social and political transformation requires a kind of practice that is linked to a sense of personal, everyday ethical practice. Unfortunately, this has often slipped through the cracks in contemporary feminist practice and social activism. The dailiness of ethical practice does not, after all, contain the visible grandeur of more formal types of activism and practice. It is perhaps ironic that the feminist goal of making women visible—in history, in politics, in society—may lead feminists to overlook the invisible everyday practices we engage in as we negotiate our lives, our jobs and our activist endeavors. Yet at an individual level it is this very quest for visibility that often compromises the ethical basis for feminist practice. I am not suggesting, of course, that women be relegated once again to the private, hidden sphere of social life or even that women or feminists should avoid positions of leadership or authority; in fact, one of the deepest necessities of ethical action may involve a willingness to take on the responsibilities of a more public form of leadership. The quest for visibility is a much deeper ethical problem and is distinct from the act of taking on a role of public responsibility. For instance, the dynamics of this desire for visibility may be manifested in the subtle investments of power that are present in the implicit sentiments of superiority that can shape individual attitudes or permeate both academic and activist progressive organizations. Such sentiments operate through "structures of recognition" in progressive networks. Visibility or recognition operates as a kind of currency which individuals aspire to gain.

This process is particularly subtle because progressive organizations often reject the conventional forms of power and authority that structure more mainstream institutions and, in doing so, often give up certain kinds of privilege. However, these organizations often operate with their own internal investments of power that can transform activism into yet another form of social capital. One of the important insights of Foucault is a stark vision of the ways in which power and resistance are inextricably linked; what we view as acts of resistance against particular structures or inequalities may actually inadvertently reproduce other, new forms of power. Resistance itself, Foucault argues, is implicated in the relationships of power we may be seeking to change.[15] While building on this approach, I also want to move beyond its limits. These limits are evidenced in the inability of Foucault and scholars building on Foucault's work to address the possibilities of transformation beyond such constraints of power. Postmodern thinkers often miss the ways in which it is and always has been possible to develop forms of transformative practice that transcend the cycle of power and resistance.

FROM ETHICAL ACTION TO SPIRITUALIZED PRACTICE

The notion of ethical action as the basis for any kind of social activism or feminist practice is a first step towards a break from this dilemma of power and resistance. However, to initiate this break we must define ethical action in a way that encompasses our entire range of practices, from our public social and political activism to a deepest sense of daily practice. For example, when I speak of the operation of such hierarchies and relationships of power in organizations I am not speaking simply of the institutional need to assign different tasks, roles and responsibilities of decision-making to individuals or committees and which may be necessary for organizations to function efficiently. I am speaking of a deeper kind of hierarchy where leadership is assumed to connote status and superiority. What is needed here is the development of a feminist approach to leadership which is based more centrally on qualities such as humility and tolerance; where visibility is a tactic rather than an end; where leadership is understood more appropriately as a form of labor and service rather than in terms of achievement. It is here that we see the ethical component of practice begin to give way to a wider, spiritualized understanding of practice. For a transition in the ways in which leadership operates is linked as much to an attitude of the spirit as it is to one's public and visible actions.

While ethical action is a necessary first step in breaking from power-laden modes of resistance, if we are to enact the broadest kind of social, political and economic transformation which feminists and other social activists have often espoused, we will need to simultaneously engage in a spiritual transformation. This possibility is not of course easily brought up with audiences of feminist and progressive intellectuals and activists in the United States. In his work on Tibetan Buddhism, the spiritual teacher Sogyal Rinpoche, noting the disturbing lack of spiritual help for the dying in the West, provides a challenging proposition. "Spiritual care" he proposes, "is not a luxury for a few; it is *the* essential right of every human being, as essential as political liberty, medical assistance, and equality of opportunity. A real democratic ideal would include knowledgeable spiritual care for everyone as one of its most essential truths."[16] Such a proposition is only striking because of its marked absence in both modern and postmodern views of social justice. Yet it is this notion of spiritual care which must be expanded and reintegrated into notions of practice if social activism is to produce lasting social, political and economic transformation.

This spiritualization of practice should not be confused with the depoliticized, personal self-help which is sometimes present in mainstream understandings of spirituality. Nor does it have anything to do with the institutionalized traditions of organized religions that have often been central to the perpetuation of gendered hierarchies. While this terrain may appear new or foreign, history is in fact ripe with instances of feminist activists who have embodied and worked for this kind of spiritualized activism. Akasha Gloria Hull, for instance, has discussed the ways in which spirituality has formed a central foundation for the political practices and visions of social justice of well known African-American feminist writers and activists such as Toni Cade Bambara, Alexis Walker, Sonia Sanchez and many others, both known and unknown. As Hull notes, for African-American feminists, "[t]hat spirituality should be a tool for combating racism and injustice is a foundational and prevailing idea."[17] Such an approach is part of a long history in which spirituality has provided the impetus for struggles against racial and gender oppression and has been embodied in the lives of central historical feminist activists such as Sojourner Truth.[18] This kind of transformative practice was also embedded in the life and work of Audre Lorde. In the challenges she posed to feminists and activists, she was never simply talking about a question of tactics, of, for example, choosing whether to work within existing institutional systems; she was advocating a revolutionary way of life, a different kind of passionate politics. As she put it, "the dichotomy between the spiritual and political is also false, resulting from an incomplete attention to our erotic knowledge. For the bridge that connects them is formed by the erotic—the sensual—those physical, emotional and psychic expressions of what is deepest and strongest and richest within each of us, being shared: the passion of love, in its deepest meanings."[19] Her writings and activism, while engaged in combating structures of racism, sexism, homophobia and class inequality, continually crossed the boundaries between spirituality, passion and politics.[20] More recently, such a spiritualized approach can be seen in the writing and lives of many of the contributors of the feminist anthology *This Bridge We Call Home.* As AnaLouise Keating notes in the introduction, "This is spirituality for social change, spirituality that recognizes the many differences among us yet insists on our commonalities and uses these commonalities as catalysts for transformation."[21] Viewed in this perspective, the writing and activist lives of such feminists represented in *This Bridge We Call Home* present concrete examples of alternative forms of leadership and the possibilities of the kind of spiritualized practice I have been discussing.

What would the beginnings of such a spiritualization of practice look like? As I've already suggested, a first small step at the individual level is simply re-linking our ideas of social activism and our quests for social justice with qualities such as compassion, humility and love.[22] This might sound simplistic in a world where we face vast problems of poverty, war and social oppression. Certainly if compassion and humility are viewed as abstract ideals they sound like another convenient slogan or theoretical idea. However, if social activism is ever to be transformative in any lasting way then qualities such as compassion and humility must be understood not as feelings or even ideas but as actual practices, practices that are a necessary component of this transformative social activism. Such a proposition may raise skepticism in the minds of some. I suggest in this case a simple test of the proposition: take a day out of your life and practice compassion and humility in every action that you take and in every thought that crosses your mind. The enormous difficulty of such a challenge only begins to reveal how much work is necessary to realize visions of social, political and economic transformation. I have so far talked about the challenge of spiritualized practice in terms of everyday practices. These are the building blocks which can then be applied to broader questions of social justice. Let us consider then how we can take this challenge beyond the individual.

BEYOND RETRIBUTION:
The Transformative Possibilities of Non-Violence

A fundamental aspect of this kind of spiritualized practice, one which necessitates a break from many existing approaches to social activism, is that it is not reserved for one's friends and comrades in struggle but also for those individuals and groups that occupy positions of power and serve to perpetuate the very structures of oppression that we may be attempting to dismantle. This philosophy of action is of course not new. In earlier times we have seen it in the kinds of non-violent resistance which activists such as Gandhi and Martin Luther King, Jr., practiced. However, the deeper spiritual meaning behind these movements has often been lost in the public memory. Currently, non-violence is mistakenly reduced to a question of tactics, a method that can be adopted as a strategy of protest in select situations. Proponents and critics usually debate when and whether non-violence can be used as an effective tactic of action. In such debates, the practice of non-violence has also often been confused with conventional ideas of pacifism. For instance, turning Mahatma Gandhi's philosophy and practice of non-violent "satyagraha," the force of truth, into the notion of "passive resistance" misses the actively transformative foundation of the kind of action he advocated; passive resistance, according to Gandhi, was "a weapon of the weak."[23] In fact, Gandhi was very clear in his writings that the practice of non-violence was a way of life, not just a choice of tactics in a larger political struggle.[24] As he put it, "non-violence of the strong cannot be a mere policy. It must be a creed or a passion."[25]

There are numerous instances of practices of non-violent activism which embody Gandhi's vision of satyagraha. In India, many social movements struggling against gender, class and caste inequality have explicitly invoked this approach. Moreover, women activists have often occupied visible leadership roles in these movements. Consider for instance the highly visible and effective social movement the Narmada

Bachao Andolan (Campaign to Save the Narmada), led by activist Medha Patkar and aimed against the construction of the large Narmada Dam in Gujarat, a state in western India.[26] The dam project has been a highly controversial project for a number of reasons. Most significantly, the dam threatened to displace villagers whose homes would be submerged by water—a situation that would deprive thousands of villagers and migrant workers of their homes and livelihood without any assurance of compensation. Critics of the dam pointed to the fact that such large-scale development projects have usually been slanted towards benefitting more privileged groups, especially in urban areas, while depriving the affected rural villagers of even a basic means of sustenance. In an ongoing struggle, activists, led by Patkar, have devoted their lives to the movement and have used methods of non-violent resistance including strategies in which those affected by the dam have refused to vacate their villages despite the threat of being drowned.[27]

Such instances of non-violent resistance are not, however, limited to India. Consider for instance the use of various forms of non-violent resistance in the context of the Israeli-Palestinian conflict, strategies which rarely gain any attention in mainstream media coverage of the accelerating cycles of violence in this region. These strategies have taken a variety of forms. Take for example the "Women in Black" movement, founded in Israel in 1988, in which women dressed in black have mourned both Palestinian and Israeli victims of violence by keeping a one-hour vigil every Friday for the past fifteen years.[28] The significance of this form of activism is underlined by its spread, as Women in Black has been transformed into a global movement with organizations struggling against war in numerous countries in Asia, Europe and the United States. Or, consider an example of activism by an Israeli organization, "Rabbis for Human Rights," that has used teachings from Jewish texts to develop a spiritual understanding and basis for non-violent activism conducted in solidarity with Palestinians in order to protest the Israeli occupation of the West Bank and Gaza. As part of its "Olive Trees Campaign," for example, the organization has planted olive trees in response to the Israeli security forces and citizens who have cut down thousands of olive trees owned by Palestinians.[29] Such instances begin to provide a sense of the possibilities of a spiritualized practice of non-violence.

Let us consider further what it means to speak of non-violence as a spiritualized practice. For instance, what does it mean to distinguish between the practice of non-violence as a method and as a way of life? The difference rests on the question of what we define as the goals of the activism we engage in. If the objective is viewed in narrowly defined material terms then the practice of non-violence may in fact not make sense. For example, if the goal is purely to seize power or material resources from an individual or group that is perpetuating unjust and oppressive structures of power, then non-violence as a method may not prove to be an effective means of action in the short term. There are countless cases in history where war or violent resistance have been successful in overcoming an enemy or oppressive force. These are the situations that critics who belittle the practice of non-violence usually point to. But their criticisms only hold up when non-violence is being treated as a simple method or tactic to pursue a particular, bounded material goal. This has nothing to do with the kind of philosophy and practice of non-violence which Gandhi, for instance, advocated in response to British colonialism in India. To speak of non-violence as a way of life, as a passion, is to base one's practice and activism on an understanding of the fundamental connections between the material (political, economic, social, cultural) and spiritual realms.[30] In his practice of non-violence, Gandhi never made a distinction between his material and spiritual objectives, a distinction which has erroneously been presumed both by leaders and activists who shared his vision of India's liberation from colonial rule and by contemporary skeptics of his philosophy of non-violence.[31] For Gandhi, a strategy of social activism that violated his spiritual principles of non-violence could never lead to a transformative form of social justice, even if this activism led to short-term material gains. This can be seen even in his early years of activism in South Africa when he refused to collaborate with forms of political resistance such as workers' protests which engaged in violence of any form.[32]

This spiritualized approach to non-violent activism in India is in many ways closer to the history of feminism in the United States than one might think. For instance, there are important parallels between the Gandhian approach and early struggles for women's rights in Europe and the United States that were connected to Quaker beliefs in non-violence and social equality originating as early as the seventeenth century.[33] Quaker practices that broke with dominant codes included having women serve as ministers, protesting war, struggling for the abolition of slavery and supporting equal rights for women. Furthermore, while the mainstream history of U.S. feminism usually places a great deal of emphasis on the struggle for women's suffrage, the spiritual dimensions of the struggles of many well-known feminist historical figures has often been written out of this history. Such spiritual traditions of activism have continued into more recent times, shaping women's non-violent protests against the Vietnam war and U.S. militarism. As with all of the examples I have pointed to, such women activists persisted despite violent and repressive responses to their struggles,[34] dispelling any false assumption that the practice of non-violence is a tool of the weak or passive.

One of the deepest foundations of this philosophy of action is that it is a form of practice that actively breaks from any desire for retributive justice. It is here that we begin to see the move beyond a narrower ethical form of practice to a broader spiritualized understanding of non-violence that rests on principles of love, compassion and forgiveness to all, including those who commit injustice. Such principles require that we leave behind any desire for retribution. It is a non-retributive understanding of justice that is necessary for any lasting transformative change; a kind of revolutionary activism which breaks from conflict-oriented models which explicitly or implicitly permeate a large portion of leftist and feminist social thought and activism. I am thinking for instance of traditional Marxist views on capitalism that are based on an analysis of the conflicts of interest between workers and capitalists. Or feminist analyses of patriarchy which focus on the conflicts of interest between men and women. Of course, material hierarchies and conflicts over power and control do exist between these groups. However, any form of activism that solely focuses on material conflicts of interest between two groups cannot make the kind of break necessary for transformative politics. In a broader spiritual sense, conflicts of interest do not exist. It is this understanding of the spiritual interdependence we all have with each other that is at the basis of a spiritualized practice of non-violence. From such a view, any act that harms another in a material sense is also spiritually damaging to the person engaging in the act. Moreover, any form of political practice that engages in violence or personal harm to another in fact only ends up mirroring the spiritual and material violence of the oppressor and ultimately cannot lead to a deeper transformative justice.

The dangers of justice based on retribution of course abound throughout history. One need only look at the ways in which Marxism, a theory grounded in a deeply egalitarian notion of justice and socioeconomic transformation, in practice turned into deeply oppressive states in the former Soviet Union and Eastern Europe. Activists and intellectuals on the left have too easily glossed over such issues. While the history and trajectories of socialist states in the former Soviet Union and currently in China and Cuba are clearly complex, we should, nevertheless, consider the inability of some of the greatest Marxist and socialist theorists and activists to really envision the practices needed to govern a radically transformed state. Marx's own original vision of communism was one which, I believe, rested on a vision that hierarchies between workers and capitalists would be transcended, leading to a just and egalitarian society. The flaw in this revolutionary project is less with the utopianism of Marx's vision than with the inability of those who built on his work to understand that an attempt to base one's vision of justice on a narrowly-defined realm of material analysis (that is, of the economic exploitation of workers) simply lacks the ethical and spiritual foundations necessary to construct an alternative kind of state.[35] Despite their radical visions for a revolutionary society, some of the most well-known thinkers have never been able to speak to the kinds of practical changes that would lead to this alternative state.[36] Hence, when socialism has been put into practice it has simply been reduced to a question of one group seizing power and resources from another group; a process which, while it does redress and reverse some material hierarchies, leaves the underpinnings of hierarchy untouched.

This example of resisting class inequality points to the unending cycles of retribution that often underlie conflict-based forms of activism and, I believe, reveals the importance of using a practice of non-violence in order to make a break from movements that seek justice through retribution. This break is critical because it marks the difference between activism that is oppositional and activism that is transformational. Consider the case of peaceful forms of anti-war resistance. Anti-war protests can have very real effects on the course of an impending or current war. Such oppositional activity can lead to important outcomes, as many anti-war protests have throughout history. However, if anti-war resistance is founded on a deeper spiritual basis that breaks with even subtle forms of retribution (such as demonizing opponents) the resistance becomes transformational because it challenges the material form of violence associated with war without producing any spiritual form of violence or injury. This kind of practice moves beyond simply opposing the immediate, visible war and transforms its underlying foundation of violence.

In the world in which we currently live, the kind of transformative social justice which a practice of non-violence seeks has never been more difficult or more necessary. This need is visibly apparent in the unending cycles of violence that have become an everyday part of life for people in regions racked by conflicts over land, territory and political independence in South Asia, the Middle East, Eastern Europe and Africa. However, the notion of retributive justice has also become globalized in the current preoccupation with terrorism and, in particular, with U.S. responses to the 9/11 terrorist attacks. There is no better example of retributive justice than the public political rhetoric of retaliation in the name of justice in the U.S. "war against terrorism." It is not coincidental that the military campaign against Afghanistan was initially called "Infinite Justice."

Both the attacks and the U.S. military responses in Afghanistan have put feminists and traditional leftists in an increasingly defensive posture as they struggle to construct a viable public alternative in the face of encroachments on civil rights, widespread nationalist fears and sentiments, vast forms of military expansion and an increasing public comfort with racial profiling and state intrusions into civil society. The type of traditional anti-war rhetoric usually derived from anti-Vietnam war protests in the 1960s has not been able to adequately address the specificities of the current situation because of the very real tragedy of the impact of the attack on civilians within the territorial boundaries of the United States and the deeply retrograde conservatism of the Islamic fundamentalism promoted by the Taliban and al Qaeda. Analyses from intellectuals on the ideological left have been able to provide important critical analyses of U.S. foreign and economic policy that can point to some of the causes of popular anti-American sentiment, and feminist analyses have been able to give us a great deal of insight into the gendered and racial implications of the current "war on terrorism" as dark-skinned Arab and South Asian immigrant men have become constructed in the public mind as potential terrorists and as a particular masculinized representation of national heroism has been glorified in the aftermath of the attacks.

Yet such criticisms are not enough to provide a strong foundation for an alternative kind of response. Moreover, the dynamics of post-9/11 United States cannot simply be reduced to discourses of race and gender, for the current threat of terrorism is a real one and the fear which people feel is also real. If progressive activist-thinkers gloss over this reality they will not be able to reach a wider public base. The difficulty at hand is to provide a courageous alternative at precisely the point when individuals feel their own personal safety is most at risk, for it is usually at this point of perceived vulnerability that we are most willing to put up our fences, lash out at others and forsake our deepest ideals, a fact witnessed by the easy way in which the American public has been willing to forsake its principles of civil liberties.[37]

In the aftermath of 9/11, media reports and commentators held up the attacks as evidence of the naiveté of philosophies of non-violence. The current climate in the United States in many ways echoes the climate of the world; it is a climate which espouses a philosophy of "any means necessary" for dominant nation-states to defend against real or perceived threats to their material security. As the U.S. has expanded its war on terrorism beyond Afghanistan to an ongoing imperial military project on a global scale, this is vividly captured in the U.S. government's doctrine of "pre-emptive war." Yet it is precisely at the moment of a threat to one's material security that a spiritualized practice of non-violent transformation is most acutely needed. The question of security in fact poses the deepest possible spiritual challenge to individuals, communities and nations—for it is an area which has created the most distortion around the meaning of self-preservation. From a spiritual perspective, any act that causes harm to another can never ultimately be an act of self-preservation. The preservation of self and security can never be founded on a conflict-oriented model of life. Nor can fences of barbed wire, fearsome military weapons and sophisticated methods of surveillance provide security. Rather, a principled philosophy of non-violence can provide an alternative path for social activism. However, this is not an alternative where we can pick and choose which kinds of violence we agree with and which kinds we condemn; to do so is to risk committing a grave spiritual error. The fact that the American media and mainstream public opinion can condemn the acts that caused the tragic deaths of thousands of civilians in the United States but not condemn the acts that subsequently caused the deaths of thousands of Iraqi soldiers and civilians in the 2003 military invasion of Iraq is a large instance of such a spiritual error. It is an error which is compounded by the assumption (reflected in public discourses) that while humanitarian concerns about Iraqi civilians are legitimate, the deaths of Iraqi soldiers are in some way justifiable.[38]

If our social activism is to be transformative, we must base it on the ethical and spiritual principles of non-violent transformation and then stand up for justice based on this foundation. The opposite—that is, to pick one's political and social goals and then decide how non-violence can fit in as a method—does not conform to the kind of transformative practice of non-violence which is now necessary. An example of this kind of principled, non-violent action can be seen in the organization "Peaceful Tomorrows," founded by some of the families of victims of the September 11th attacks.[39] One of the principles underlying their work has been to transform their own suffering and loss into a basis for working towards non-violent responses to terrorism. They have focused on various issues including working with victims of the U.S. bombing in Afghanistan and protesting the war with Iraq. Such work provides an important example of the ways in which individuals' real suffering provided the basis for a transformative response that broke with cycles of violent retribution.

I am not suggesting or assuming for a moment that this is an easy strategy. Consider, for instance, what it entails if non-violence is to truly be a way of life rather than simply a policy or method to be used when convenient or effective. At a larger political scale, it means rejecting those violent actions and beliefs of oppressed social groups that we may sympathize with. It means speaking out and acting against injustice without causing personal harm to those who are perpetuating the acts. It means extending compassion and forgiveness to those we perceive to be oppressors. And, finally, it means extending these practices to every interaction in our everyday lives. Too often it is assumed that violence is only constituted by acts that cause physical injury to others and that non-violent resistance entails public acts such as the kinds civil disobedience advocated by leaders such as Gandhi and Martin Luther King, Jr. Unfortunately, violence is a much broader phenomenon that includes the kind of harm caused by hate speech, ill will or personal animosities. A recognition of the normalized dailiness of such violence must be a component of any form of non-violent activism. Feminists and other social activists have recognized these daily acts of violence when they have, for example, called attention to the damage caused by certain kinds of hate speech based on racial, ethnic or gendered discrimination. But what has often not been recognized is the ways in which this normalized violence creeps into our everyday actions and behaviors in ways that are not reducible to questions of structured inequalities such as race or gender. Consider for instance the forms of retaliation that occur between peers in workplace situations or the pervasiveness of slander that may circulate amongst "progressive" intellectuals and activists who espouse public social justice but compete with one another in their quests for visibility and power within organizations and institutions. These patterns of behavior point to what Martin Luther King, Jr., called the "the internal violence of the spirit."[40] This is not of course to imply that ethical behavior is absent in such arenas but to point to the strong potential for the corruption of the transformative potential of social activism when a false dichotomy between public activism and private everyday behavior is assumed. It is, after all, easier to condemn public physical violence that others engage in than to conduct a self-examination of one's own practices, both at the individual and collective levels.

THE PRACTICAL MEANING OF REDEMPTIVE SUFFERING

As I have said, no one should assume that this kind of practice is an easy process. One of the most demanding aspects of the practice of non-violence has to do with the question of suffering. The depth and vastness of suffering caused by poverty, war and various forms of abuse and social oppression is perhaps one of the most difficult issues one must face when advocating principles of non-violence. It is, after all, much easier to espouse such principles at the level of abstraction than when a loved one has been killed, when a military attack has destroyed one's home or simply when one suffers from the violence of desperate levels of poverty and deprivation while others consume the products of your labor and inhabit lives of material privilege. Yet it is precisely when it comes to the question of suffering that we come to the heart of the meaning of active non-violence. As Martin Luther King, Jr., explained,

> ...suffering can be a most creative and powerful force...Now it is very interesting at this point that both violence and non-violence agree that suffering can be a very powerful social force. But there is this difference: violence says that suffering can be a powerful social force by inflicting the suffering on somebody else: so this is what we do in war, this is what we do in the whole violent thrust of the violent movement. It believes that you achieve some end by inflicting suffering on another. The non-violent say that suffering becomes a powerful social force when you willingly accept that violence on yourself, so that self-suffering stands at the center of the non-violent movement and the individuals involved are able to suffer in a creative manner, feeling that unearned suffering is redemptive, and that suffering may serve to transform the social situation.[41]

The kind of redemptive suffering that King describes is radically different from the passive suffering which an individual or social group might experience from remaining in or acquiescing to abuse or oppression. It should not be mistaken for an acceptance or preservation of the status quo or of any form of injustice, nor is this an otherworldly idea which suggests that women (or men) must suffer quietly in their oppression and wait for their redemption beyond this world. This clarification is particularly important from a feminist perspective, as the idea of the silent, self-sacrificing woman has often provided the ideological means for curtailing women's freedom and power. In fact, redemptive suffering provokes and demands the opposite of such patriarchal constructions.

A striking example of the use of redemptive suffering as a source of activism can be seen in a long history of resistance to military rule in El Salvador from the 1970s to the 1990s. During this period, social activists and El Salvadoran civilians (particularly those from poor communities) who were caught in the midst of the violent civil war between the El Salvadorian state and organized resistance to it faced extreme levels of state repression, including the widespread use of torture and the "disappearance" of activists as well as of individuals simply caught in the midst of the conflict. In this conflict, a spiritualized form of resistance became a central means of opposing the military regime as civilians, grassroots activists, nuns and male clergy broke with the conservative formal structures of the church (whose leadership supported the military regime) and put into practice a form of liberation theology that was defined by its opposition both to the violence of the military regime as well as the structural violence against the poor. Spirituality in this case was located in the act of working for and with the poor against such violence.[42] A central figure in this resistance was Archbishop Oscar Romero, who preached and practiced a form of spiritualized non-violence that grew increasingly threatening to the military regime because of its popular support and mobilizational effectiveness. However, as Dennis, Golden and Wright have suggested in their biography of Romero, this form of spiritualized politics cannot be reduced to the traditional view of an individual leader preaching to the masses. In fact, such activism drew on grassroots understandings of spirituality as *mistica*, the spirit of community.[43]

Consider just one example of this form of redemptive spiritual transformation which Dennis, Golden and Wright describe,

> When farmworkers, union organizers, or members of the Christian base communities in El Salvador gather to commemorate the heroism of their people, they enact a liturgy of memory that has profound creative power. The names of those who were killed in the service of liberation are called out, and after each name the community exuberantly shouts, *¡Presente!* The dead are truly present in the community. They

are present not simply by virtue of their claim that life is more than self-fulfillment; they are present in that space where life is held sacred. This holding of life as sacred, as imbued with *mistica*, is not rhetorical but a daily creative task. In a culture of death, where death by torture, poverty, or cynicism and despair, the task of keeping open the space for *mistica*—for life itself and the hope for life—belongs to those whose power derives from their spirit of resistance.[44]

This practice of reading out the names of the murdered and disappeared was carried out in the midst of acute military repression and was viewed by the El Salvadorian state as a political act of subversion; the redemption of the dead was literally brought about by rendering "present" those who had been murdered; they were given life as their memory became a spiritual basis for the continued struggle against the regime. Such forms of redemptive spiritualized politics can also be seen in organizations specifically involving women activists in El Salvador. For instance, the organization "Mothers of the Disappeared" transformed such acts of witnessing and memory into direct confrontations with the government by demanding information about their relatives and friends who had been seized by the state.[45] Such examples of women's activism in the face of acute ideological and physical coercion (the Mothers were declared by the state to be terrorists and individual activists were often beaten and severely tortured) were far from unique. Instead, they were part of a broader movement in which both individual women and nuns who broke with their orders took on grassroots activist work. As Renny Golden has noted, much of this activism led to the creation of a "popular church" that rested on a spiritualized approach to social transformation—a "church [that] is distinctive because it is a church of nonclerics, of the poor, and most of the local pastoral leadership is women."[46]

The case of El Salvador is a striking example of the power of redemptive suffering because of the extent of repression that activists faced in their struggle. It is an important example because it demonstrates the practical significance of the kind of spiritualized practice I have been discussing and cautions against a dismissal of this practice as too saintly or removed from "real" political issues. Redemptive suffering in fact is not a special power that more visible leaders such as Romero, Gandhi or King possessed. It is a resource that all individuals can draw on and, as the case of El Salvador demonstrates, it can provide a particularly important foundation for the activism of marginalized social groups and grassroots activists.

There are many ways in which this process can be understood. But at the simplest level it involves reaching deep inside the pain and suffering within oneself and transforming that suffering into a source of empowerment and transformation. This is one of the oldest practices in any social justice movement. For instance, feminists and activists struggling for racial justice have long discussed the "double vision" of oppressed groups, that is, the ways in which experiences of oppression provide individuals and groups with a kind of "second sight" that gives them the tools to analyze structures of oppression and the vision to see the possibilities of a world free from such oppression.[47] Yet this approach involves more than simply gaining an understanding of the nature of oppression and injustice; it also involves using one's suffering as the guide and basis for activism. What makes this kind of practice transformative is how it enables one to break out of the cycle of violence that is inherent in any form of justice based on retribution, no matter how subtle the retribution may seem. In this process, the individuals or groups practicing non-violence make a fundamental break from the logic of oppression.

This process will not make sense if viewed in narrowly defined material or political terms where it is assumed that power and justice are based purely on seizing control, nor if our understandings of self-interest rest on beliefs of a bounded material self divorced from a spiritual self. For from such a viewpoint it would of course not make sense to withstand more suffering in order not to inflict harm on the perpetrators. It only makes sense if we define liberation in terms that include the economic, political, social and the spiritual dimensions of our lives and our selves. For the practice of non-violence is the spiritualization of suffering. It is founded on the understanding of the immeasurable spiritual damage that an act of violence causes the perpetrator. It is founded on an understanding of the deep wells of spiritual strength that are necessary for victims of oppression to break out of cycles of violence in ways that can be truly transformative. It is founded on a recognition that, in spiritual terms, there is no distinction between the means we use and the ends we seek. It is founded on an understanding of a form of transformation that involves the liberation of both the oppressed and the perpetrators of oppression. For the practice of non-violence demands that activists struggle against all forms of injustice and hierarchy without reproducing a conflict-oriented model of the world. Suffering became a "creative force" for someone like Martin Luther King, Jr., because it opened him and his vision of racial justice up in ways that encompassed the suffering and needs of all of humanity. It is important to note that this is not the same as a liberal approach to politics which assumes that we can all come to the conference table, "set aside our differences" and engage in a dialogue. A spiritualized view of suffering does not mean that material inequalities magically disappear. And in most cases, non-violent practice does not immediately reach the hearts and minds of those who perpetuate social oppression; usually those who have privileges will lash out even more in order to cling to them.

FEMINISM AS GIVING

Such reflections on the practice of non-violence, it is clear, necessitate a significant rethinking of many characteristics of contemporary social activism in general and of feminist practice in particular. Contemporary feminism has been primarily framed in terms of demands for equality—demands usually made on the state or on social and political institutions. Such demands are, of course, a necessary part of a broader movement for social justice. However, the exclusive focus on demands has led feminists to miss another equally important focus, a focus on the process of giving and of giving up. What would feminism look like if it paid attention to both what it needs to ask for and what it needs to give up? The question is particularly salient for those of us who hold privileges of various forms. In fact, some of the intense internal debates that have emerged within contemporary feminism have really been about challenging feminists to deal with precisely this question. I am thinking, for instance, of the numerous challenges that women of color have presented to white women regarding the racialized exclusions that have permeated feminism as well as the challenges of Third World feminists to Western feminists and their relationship to the agendas and ideologies of their governments.[48] These are examples of challenges to more privileged groups of women to give up control of agendas, organizations, resources and fields of knowledge so that feminism can be transformed into a more genuinely inclusive movement. It is simply an expanded understanding of this process of giving up that forms the counterpoint to the conventional feminist focus on making demands.

When we think of feminism in this way, then marginalized groups of women who challenge women in more privileged racial, national or socioeconomic locations are no longer seen as divisive. Furthermore, if "giving up" is seen as a central tenet of feminism, then differences between women need not be a source of anguish. This anguish has been a common refrain in Women's Studies, usually (but not always) from more privileged women who ask, "If we keep focusing on differences how can we be unified enough to act?" The assumption that a focus on inequalities between women is an obstacle to activism stems from an incomplete understanding of practice. This process is of course not unique to feminism. It is symptomatic of many traditional forms of social activism and movements; consider, for instance, the historical resistance of the traditional "left" to a focus on issues of gender difference. The problem is not with the question of difference. It is one of understanding that activism involves two simultaneous processes: making demands and giving up.

The principles of sacrifice—of giving up—that are inherent within a spiritualized practice of non-violence can also be applied to the smaller, local sense of daily life. There is currently a great deal of talk about the processes of globalization, which have been breaking down the economic and cultural boundaries between peoples, nations and cultures. However, this interest has not really translated into an everyday consciousness of what globalization means for the ways in which we live our lives, that is, a consciousness of how even our smallest actions affect the rest of the world. This consciousness is particularly important when it comes to our lifestyles and our everyday practices of consumption. Those who are committed to feminism in the U.S. must face the fact that the clothes we buy are usually manufactured by underpaid women who work in the garments industry in countries such as Bangladesh, India or Indonesia. This is true even if we choose not to practice extravagant forms of consumption because discount stores are also stocked with such "cheaply manufactured" products. Or, consider the act of driving a car. I live in New Jersey, a place which is steeped in a culture of driving; the excessive driving which I must do simply to go about my daily life is directly linked to broader processes of environmental degradation which affect the entire world. There are an infinite number of such examples; it is this enormity of the overlapping and interconnected structures that shape the most intimate and minute fabric of our lives that can lead to a form of paralysis.

How do we circumvent such large economic structures when most of us have no immediate control over the actions of wealthy corporations and the vested political interests that support them? It is not possible to find a space of pure innocence outside of the current structures of global capitalism. While it is possible to engage in a more critical reflection of our consumption practices, the solution is also not necessarily one of embracing the kind of extreme asceticism that Gandhi advocated; extreme asceticism can itself turn into a form of violence against one's own self, particularly when it stems from feelings of guilt. Self-blame on the one hand and personal condemnations of others' lifestyles on the other are both strategies of the ego. Both evade responsibility: the first by assuming that the structures are too large to even attempt to change anything; the second by focusing on the personal failings of others, thus enabling a false sense of superiority, a kind of self-valorization that forecloses our own processes of self-examination.

Instead of leading to self-blame or personal condemnations, a recognition of our implication in the exploitation of others and of the global environment can be deeply productive when it serves to infuse our lives and activism with both a real sense of humility and the courage to work for real social change. When we begin to discover and build on real humility in our selves and in our activism, we have, in effect, begun the transformative process. It is only here that we can begin to develop a foundation for the practice of the non-violence of the spirit, a lasting form of transformative action that is not stunted by the illusory distinctions between the means we use and the ends we seek, between the public and the private, the spiritual and the material, the dailiness of our everyday lives and the grander actions that we classify as social activism.

Throughout this discussion I have moved from the smallest examples of everyday life to the largest kinds of social movements for non-violent transformation in order to underline the dynamic and ongoing nature of the practice of non-violence. However, these principles do not provide a twelve-step program on how to be an activist or build an activist organization. The concrete actions each of us take will vary depending on our lives, our circumstances, our capacity to believe in change. In fact, I have deliberately wanted to decenter the product-oriented understanding of activism which assumes that practice begins with and is embodied by formal organizations. Organizations, of course, are a necessary method for carrying out various forms of service and activism. However, when they become the endpoint rather than a limited vehicle that grows out of a broader understanding of practice we are left with an overabundance of centers, institutes and organizations of various kinds that eventually outlive the spirit of activist transformation they are built with.[49]

For those who are committed to a broad and lasting form of societal transformation, a philosophy and practice of non-violence can serve as both the means and the end. Let us not turn the very meaning of practice on its head by reflexively asserting that non-violence as activism and as a way of life is impractical. Transformative action *is* a utopian project. However, a spiritualized understanding of social justice recognizes that utopias are not simply noble goals, they are realizable possibilities. Such principles of the practice of non-violence are, I have come to believe, the building blocks for a humble yet unstoppable form of transformation in a world that grows dangerously desperate for an alternative state of being.

Chapter 4 **Knowledge**

What is the role of knowledge in the struggle for social transformation? What kinds of understandings are included in our definitions of "knowledge"? How must these definitions be challenged and remade if we are to transform knowledge from a means of maintaining domination into a kind of liberatory practice? These are old questions. Yet they are questions that continue to provoke intense debates with tremendous stakes because how and what we know is implicated within complicated sets of political and economic interests. Within the academy there has been a great deal of writing on how knowledge reproduces, and is embedded within, larger relationships of power. Feminist and postcolonial scholars have, for example, shown the ways in which the creation of knowledge about societies colonized by Europe in the eighteenth and nineteenth centuries was both shaped by and used as a tool to further the process of colonization.[1] For example, feminists have shown that colonial knowledge about "cultural traditions" that sanctioned violence against women such as female infanticide or sati (widow burning) in India in fact often participated in inventing these traditions or making them more rigid.[2] European colonial officers and intellectuals depicted specific acts of violence against women in non-Western societies as symbolic of their cultural traditions, and used such acts to justify the need for the civilizing forces of colonial rule. Meanwhile, as I have noted in earlier chapters, feminist scholars have also demonstrated the ways in which such dynamics occur in current times, as mainstream Western discourses represent practices such as veiling and dowry deaths as symbols of the cultural backwardness of "Third World" countries. There is now a rich body of scholarship that has examined these dynamics. This scholarship questions the innocence of knowledge that claims to describe the oppression of subjugated non-Western social groups, suggesting that knowledge itself has historically served as a tool of colonialism and other forms of domination.

Such trends in the academy have provided important tools to take apart stereotypes and forms of knowledge that reproduce power and dominance. However, what has been missing in this endeavor is sufficient attention to the possibilities of producing knowledge is not trapped by such questions of power. Students in the classroom are shortchanged when they are not given the tools, or even the belief, that they can learn and know in ways that do not simply replicate oppressive structures. In this situation, students are either limited to the project of deconstruction (where they learn to criticize or unpack the power relations inherent in different forms of representation such as film, media images and literary and scholarly texts) or they rebel against such an approach and return to a more conventional approach to knowledge—as an objective realm that is not steeped in relationships of power. This divergence has often been mistaken in Women's Studies as a divide between theory and practice, "theory" being a sign for a deconstructive understanding of power and knowledge and "practice" being a sign for the demand for "straightforward" or "objective" empirical descriptions of women's activism or, in some cases, a sign for the rejection of knowledge as irrelevant to "real life." The irony is that both sides of this false opposition impoverish the possibilities of knowledge.

My objective in this chapter is to try to move beyond this impasse and to consider possibilities for the creation of transformative forms of knowledge. I draw on many of the insights of postcolonial, postmodern and feminist scholars who have made us confront the relationship between power and knowledge. They have shown us that knowledge is not a neutral entity, but a set of practices that produce relationships of power. This is a central insight that a polarized divide between "theory" and "practice" misses. I begin the chapter by briefly outlining this perspective; however, I argue for an approach that does not restrict itself to deconstruction or to an assumption that what and how we know must always be caught within hierarchical relationships of power. I focus in particular on two key issues. The first is an understanding of knowledge as a form of ethical practice that cannot be fully contained either by social scientific claims of neutrality and objectivity or by a postmodern focus on power. The second is the possibility of an approach to knowledge that draws on the spiritualized practice of non-violence which I discussed in chapter 3. In other words, when knowledge is understood as a set of practices, it is possible to apply the principles of spiritualized non-violent transformation to these "knowledge practices." I specifically examine an active form of witnessing as an example of this transformative approach to knowledge. As in the previous chapter, the discussion of the ethical component of practice is a first step that leads to and is part of a broader spiritualized approach to knowledge practices. While I focus on practices and debates within the academy, my hope is that this discussion will also be relevant to non-academic organizations that address questions of social justice. Non-academic organizations also engage in the production of knowledge, whether through the reports they write, the languages they use in their campaigns or the pictures they use in their publicity materials. In fact, many criticisms of the representation of subjugated groups such as Third World women or women of color have addressed both academic and activist representations. In my understanding, knowledge practices, in their broadest sense, are practices that activists, teachers, journalists, writers and students all engage in.

POWER, KNOWLEDGE AND THE PROBLEM OF REPRESENTATION

Let us begin with a controversy that currently preoccupies a large segment of feminists and social justice writers/activists, the question of the politics of representation, particularly the representation of less-privileged social groups. Feminist writing has undergone important shifts in the last few decades. In earlier periods, feminists pressed for the inclusion of women in studies that usually made generalizations about society based on the experiences of privileged men. Feminists demonstrated that the inclusion of women both as producers of knowledge and as subjects being studied challenged the exclusionary and gendered nature of knowledge. Such challenges were not limited to the academy as they also addressed both governmental and non-governmental organizations that had defined policies and agendas based on gendered views of the world. For example, such challenges led to broadened definitions of work to include women's employment in part-time or household work and broadened definitions of history to make visible the significance of women's activities both inside and outside the household in shaping social movements. Such strategies for inclusion also shaped the rewriting of histories from the perspectives of subordinated social groups such as workers, peasants, and various racial and ethnic communities.

However, this drive for the inclusion of the perspectives of subordinated social groups was soon questioned by scholars who called for a greater attention to the strategies of representation being used, that is, how the identities, experiences and activities of such groups were being depicted in academic texts as well as in non-academic representations used by social activists (such as film and political rhetoric). There is now a vast body of scholarship that has shown the ways in which particular strategies of representation may serve to recolonize less-privileged groups by presenting them as passive victims, devoid of agency, and by inadvertently stereotyping such groups and their cultures and nations.[3] This has of course been particularly salient in the case of social groups in the Third World or racialized ethnic groups in the advanced industrialized countries. Such scholarship has also examined the power dynamics involved when researchers intrude into the lives of less-privileged groups in order to collect data, document life histories and produce ethnographies. Anybody who has conducted fieldwork can attest to the serious ethical complications that researching and writing can produce, for the entire process of fieldwork involves intruding into people's lives, asking for their time away from overworked lives, taking their memories, their wisdom and their understanding and making it one's own property. Squarely confronting these processes, as many feminist scholars have,[4] is paralyzing enough to deter anyone from engaging in this kind of knowledge production. Indeed, I have regularly seen graduate students go into a state of panic at the thought of beginning their field-work and having to negotiate such power dynamics.[5]

Such questions of power do not, of course, disappear once the period of field research is over. Nor are they limited to those individuals who do ethnographic research; they apply whether one is writing an ethnography, doing a quantitative survey or reaching back into time and constructing histories from memories and lives organized in archives. The focus on power has tended to concentrate on those who produce films and documentaries, or write ethnographies or texts based on interviews because of the immediate and visible interactive nature of such projects. But such questions are as relevant even when it appears that one is simply working with archives and quantitative data; the lives at stake are simply better hidden in these cases.[6] They are also significant in situations when activists are from more privileged backgrounds than the communities they work with; and in a world where transnational activism is an important dimension for many organizations, they will continue to be of importance outside of the academy.

These issues inevitably seem debilitating, and have often led both students and intellectuals to reject the task of studying less-privileged social groups. It is the danger inherent in this kind of research that led Gayatri Spivak to pose her stark rhetorical question, "Can the subaltern speak?" Her response is that no, they cannot speak through our texts, that those who engage in the research are participating in the deeply colonial process of "information gathering" from "informants." Spivak's view has also influenced some critical responses to the possibilities of transnational activism. Critics have noted that colonial legacies, which I have discussed earlier, continue to shape the relationship between more privileged Western feminists and social groups and activists that live and work in less-privileged countries. For instance, transnational feminism has often focused more on cultural oppression rather than on economic and political oppression, which would require a deeper focus on the implication of U.S. policies in furthering women's oppression in the Third World.[7] Such critics have rightly pointed out that the current Western feminist concern with genital mutilation in Africa, veiling in the Middle East and Islamic world and dowry deaths in South Asia often reflect a kind of orientalist fascination that stems from the legacies of colonialism. Here, feminists are engaged in implicit knowledge practices when they claim to "know" that the causes of women's oppression are cultural. Despite the vast and growing feminist criticisms of the ways in which such issues stereotype and misrecognize the complex realities of women's lives in these regions, year after year students in Women's Studies classes remain preoccupied with them.

Given such dynamics, the response that "the subaltern cannot speak" through the layers of representation in academic texts and political rhetoric is understandable, for the power-laden dilemmas of research can indeed seem insurmountable. But this is a response which does not risk trying to find transformative possibilities for knowledge. A purely deconstructive approach to the links between power and knowledge can raise flags and point to the problems of colonizing forms of knowledge but it cannot envision a way out of these structures. In examining an alternative possibility, I want to build on rather than simply move past the important insights regarding the messy politics of representation that I have been outlining. Academics and activists, frustrated by the paralyzing debates on representation, have simply sought to ignore or dismiss these insights as "abstract theory." Too often in Women's Studies, there is a rejection of a focus on power and knowledge production, based on the assumption that it is merely academic or theoretical and not related to feminist practice.[8] Those who engage in such a rejection usually do not recognize that knowledge production itself is also a form of practice, nor do they recognize that activists outside of the academy also participate in this practice of knowledge production. What I want to explore is ways in which we can learn from these debates on the politics of representation without being trapped by them. The question then is what does one do in the face of such power dynamics? How do we respond and transform our knowledge practices? It is here that an understanding of knowledge as a form of ethical practice can begin to point to a way out of the current dilemmas of power, knowledge and representation.

KNOWLEDGE AS ETHICAL PRACTICE

What does it mean to speak of knowledge as an ethical practice? To consider knowledge as an ethical practice is to recognize and accept the power-laden relationships that permeate it without being ultimately trapped by these relationships of power. Let us begin with the question of the representation of subordinated social groups. A central dilemma that has shaped the politics of representation has had to do with how academic texts and activist organizations have represented the oppression of subordinated groups. Such questions are fundamentally linked to questions of methodology—that is, how we do our research and writing or how we work in and with communities through our activist organizations.

In the academy, methodological questions in the social sciences have usually tended to focus more on questions of objectivity and scientific rigor than on questions regarding the politics of representation. Meanwhile, feminist and postmodern criticisms have tended to focus more on the power effects of representations. I want to consider the ways in which an understanding of knowledge as ethical practice can move us beyond these oppositional poles of objectivity and power. What is needed is a form of ethical action that is embedded in practices of research and representation (the production of knowledge) as well as in practices of the consumption of knowledge (that is, how we interpret, respond to and act on the knowledge we receive). Such a move does not entail a rejection of a focus on power. Rather what I want to explore is what ethical responses to power dynamics would look like. Treating knowledge as ethical action seeks to address specific practices that could be taken to begin to make knowledge transformative. I want to consider the possibilities of thinking of knowledge practices in terms of witnessing.

The witness fundamentally differs from the objective observer/scholar because the witness consciously accepts both the power-laden relationship and the ethical responsibility of the act of witnessing.[9] If we are to transform knowledge of oppression into a liberatory act, we must begin by practicing a kind of witnessing that breaks through the traditional hierarchies and relationships of power that govern how we see. There are already long traditions of witnessing social injustice and oppression, ranging from the use of testimonials (such as *testimonio* in Latin American cultures), the practice of witnessing in Quaker communities that draw on the biblical idea of bearing witness as well as the writings of a long history of social activists who have written not as objective, detached scholars but as engaged thinkers speaking out about and against the injustices they observe.[10] In drawing inspiration from these sources, there are several key elements that I believe shape the role of the witness. First, the witness becomes implicated in the situation or form of oppression being observed; that is, the presence of the witness changes the dynamics of the situation at hand and is not simply an external observer. Second, the act of witnessing represents a learning process for the witness. The subjects being witnessed, in effect, represent the teachers in this situation; knowledge is being given to the witness. This is a departure from traditional views of the intellectual as the sole individual who knows and educates others. Shoshana Felman insightfully describes this in terms of the ways in which knowledge has the potential to serve as "testimony to an apprenticeship of history and to an apprenticeship of witnessing."[11] Drawing on a discussion of Albert Camus' *The Plague*, she describes the way that the "narrator (a 'historian,' witness of the other witnesses), *learns something* from the witnessing and from the telling."[12] Given that the witness is implicated in the situation being observed and obligated to the subjects of study, the act of witnessing brings with it a very deep form of both ethical and, as I will argue later, spiritual responsibility.

Recognizing and accepting the responsibility of witnessing through an application of practical ethical and spiritual principles can enable the production of knowledge to move beyond an exploitative form of extraction. In fact, the act of witnessing, whether embodied through our research, writing, filmmaking, journalism or simply in the everyday interactions of our lives, is one of the most potentially transformative knowledge practices we can engage in. It is transformative because the individual bearing witness is fundamentally transformed by it; this is a critical departure from how we usually think about what people are doing when they are representing "other" people. We often assume, for instance, that writing a book about a less-privileged group is engaging in an endeavor that will help the group in question, that the knowledge produced will somehow save them, that writing about the forms of power that constrain their lives will somehow change things. In actuality, academic knowledge produced about less-privileged groups rarely affects them directly.[13] In other words, the act of describing or analyzing experiences of oppression for a wider audience is not in itself necessarily transformative for the group or individuals who experience this oppression. Postmodern critics have rightly pointed out that not only does such knowledge rarely benefit its subjects, it may actually harm them through stereotyping, essentializing and colonizing strategies of representation.

The simple truth is that it is the witness describing the oppression of less-privileged groups who is most likely to undergo a transformation. But historically the potential transformation of the witness has more often than not taken the form of a kind of extraction, where the lives, cultures and struggles of different groups have provided fodder for the self-valorization and domination of the witness in question. This is what scholars like Chandra Mohanty have pointed out, arguing that Western feminists have colonized Third World women through their knowledge production. Mohanty demonstrates that by depicting Third World women as victims devoid of agency, Western feminists have instead given the power of agency to themselves. The Western feminist figure in Mohanty's analysis has been in a sense transformed by witnessing the oppression of Third World women, but this transformation has rested on a theft of agency and hence cannot ultimately provide, as Mohanty points out, a foundation for a form of liberatory knowledge.

The problem, however, is that a purely deconstructive approach leaves us at this stage, assuming for the most part that representation can never circumvent relationships of power and thus cannot provide a basis for social transformation. Individuals who persist in creating films, ethnographies, histories or even novels have responded to this dilemma in a number of ways. Many have reacted with hostility to the postmodern focus on the production of knowledge and have, unfortunately, simply ignored the links between power, knowledge and practices of representation as they have continued with their work. Others, however, have taken the challenge seriously and have attempted to subvert the power of representation. To that end they have invented a variety of strategies ranging from locating the author or filmmaker in the texts or films being produced, staging oral histories and ethnographies as dramas or fictions, or simply resorting to confessionals where the author becomes as much subject as witness. Such strategies have often been creative and have produced a rich field of feminist methodology and knowledge production. However, a rarely acknowledged aspect of such strategies is that, because they are all focused on the knower rather than the known, they are in essence techniques to cope with what it means to be a witness committed to the production of socially transformative knowledge. It is this question which I am trying to wrestle with here.

If the act of witnessing is more likely to be transformative for the witness rather than the subject, what can we do to prevent this act from remaining oriented to the self in an exploitative way, rather than to a broader process of social transformation? The act of witnessing, I have come to understand, brings with it a deep ethical responsibility. This responsibility is of course linked to the many relationships of power with which feminists and other intellectuals and activists have already struggled. But it does not have to be trapped by such relationships. For active witnessing holds within it the potential for breaking out of and transforming the existing material structures and hierarchies that weave the lives of the dominant and the less privileged together. An active form of witnessing bears with it the responsibility of upholding the kinds of ethical principles and practices which I have been reflecting on in the previous chapter. Thus, for those who engage in any kind of knowledge practices that draw on the lives and understanding of the less privileged (knowledge practices which can range from writing books to making films to crafting policy papers to putting out activist political manifestos) attending to this ethical responsibility must begin in the context where one is learning.[14] To take one simple example, it has always been remarkable to me that with all of the attention, both positive and negative, that is directed at power, knowledge and representation, Social Science departments have almost a complete absence of courses on the ethics of research. Whereas professional schools such as business schools and law schools have courses on business and legal ethics, such formal ethical guidance is almost absent in the social sciences. The result is that students have little training or time for reflection on the ethics of fieldwork and research—on the kinds of ethical principles they can bring to their interactions with individuals, institutions and the nations which they enter into on a regular basis.

Yet the process of research is fraught with ethical questions. Questions of how one gains access to information and to individuals; questions of what kinds of questions can and should be asked; questions about what kind of information the researcher should ethically provide to the subjects of the research; questions of how one uses the information obtained not just in one's writing but in the context where one is researching. The list could, of course, go on. And such questions do not even begin to touch on the daily ethical questions that come up in individual interactions as researchers negotiate with the subjects of their study.

Of course both anthropologists and feminists have spent much time considering such ethical questions. But more often than not, they address these questions in terms of power relationships between researcher and subject; relationships based on identities of race, nation, gender, sexuality and class, to name the most visibly debated. Or these questions are cast in terms of the inherent power dynamics in the process of research—a fundamental power relationship between the researcher (the knower) on the one hand and the subject (the known) on the other hand. The limitation of this focus is that one is invariably left with the recognition that power dynamics cannot be circumvented; they can be negotiated and written about, but such material hierarchies of course cannot disappear. And hence, discussions of these dynamics tend to turn either into a display of guilty hand wringing or, more commonly, into a narrow conversation about how one represents power dynamics in the texts being written (for instance, by openly talking about the researcher's location). Let us be clear, however: talking about power dynamics in one's representation can serve an important purpose in shaping how the texts we produce are consumed (by recognizing and responding to certain power dynamics through specific textual strategies). But such conversations do not address what kinds of ethical practices should be used during the process of research. The kind of ethical practices that are needed in any project of representation both inside and outside the academy cannot be reduced to a question of the textual strategies used by writers. What is missing and what is desperately needed is an explicit discussion of the ethical principles and practices that should guide our behavior during the process of our research. It is once again the dailiness of ethical action which I am talking about; here the dailiness of our actions within the villages, cities and nations which we research and analyze.

It should be immediately apparent that it would be most unlikely for all academics to agree on what constitutes ethical action in research. Consider, for instance, the question of confidentiality and the use of information one gains. What is a researcher to do when making information public may cause harm? The question may appear easy but, in fact, it is not, for it raises difficult questions of context, responsibility and the purpose of the knowledge we produce. Consider some hypothetical situations. The information in question may be provided by an individual subject in confidence to an ethnographer in the context of a friendship which may have developed during the course of research.[15] For instance, the subject may reveal having experienced a personal trauma such as domestic violence. But if this information is being revealed as an outgrowth of friendship rather than in a clear-cut interview, the act of revealing this information may represent a deep violation of trust, even if the individual is renamed and is not known by the people reading about it. This is what Kamala Visweswaran so incisively touches on when she describes the acts of betrayal that sometimes unfold in the process of field research.[16] She dramatizes an interaction which occurred during her own field research in India, where she was interviewing women who had participated in the Indian nationalist movement, in which a woman betrays her friend by revealing to Visweswaran personal information about her friend's private life which her friend had been keeping hidden. Visweswaran's quest for information about these women's lives leads to this betrayal of confidence. Visweswaran insightfully points to the ways in which the feminist quest for knowledge in this case rests not on an uncomplicated form of sisterhood but on the power relations and pain of betrayal.

While Visweswaran calls our attention to the problem of betrayal, she does not address the possibilities of an ethical response to the situation. She does not reflect on the kinds of ethical practices she should have engaged in during her encounter with the two women. Instead she fictionalizes the situation and represents the betrayal between two friends and stages a third betrayal by revealing this intimate set of interactions. In other words, while Visweswaran witnesses the betrayal she does not address the ethical implications of making public both the private information disclosed as well as the betrayal itself. Dramatizing the interaction and blurring the lines between ethnography and fiction are interesting responses to the issue of representation but they do not address what I believe is a much more fundamental question—what kinds of ethical principles should guide the researcher's interactions and use of information in such contexts? It is not enough to re-enact the dilemmas of power and representation in a fictionalized form. Fictionalizing narratives of ethnography does not change the fact that interactions and actions in the field are real. Such fictionalized strategies may be useful responses in that they challenge the readers to recognize the power dynamics of fieldwork and of our textual representations; however, they do not take the next step and provide ethical guidelines for the practice of research and writing. Nor is it enough to rely on the fact that in many cases the revelation of our subjects' lives will remain confidential because we conceal their names or because our texts written in academic English prose will not ultimately be accessible to them or to people who may know them. Ethical questions remain even in fiction and in anonymity.

I point to these dilemmas because Visweswaran's discussion is characterized by a sense of honesty that is often missing in academic writing and because it therefore comes so close to raising questions of ethical practice; that is, she demonstrates the ways in which her role as witness becomes implicated in a messy form of power and betrayal. Moreover, I do not suggest that the solution is necessarily one of silence, that is, of not revealing any information. Both silence and disclosure contain within them the risks of betrayal and the possibilities of transformation. My point is that we need to move beyond a recognition of the forms of betrayal which researchers inadvertently stage and address the principles with which to respond to these situations. Without an explicit discussion of ethical practice we cannot begin to have any sense of how to produce alternative forms of knowledge.

The question at hand then is: How do we produce knowledge about the experience and causes of oppression in ways that are non-exploitative and which do not turn people's suffering into a spectacle that we safely consume from a distance? As I have been arguing, this is a fundamentally ethical question which many writers, activists and scholars have struggled with. It raises issues which are of particular intensity now, as people's lives are increasingly shaped by a media-driven society that is founded precisely on this very process of turning suffering into spectacle. It is thus critical for writers/activists who produce and disseminate knowledge about oppression to guard against this consumption-oriented approach to suffering. The challenge is to make our acts of our representation enact a form of witnessing rather than of spectatorship. This is a difficult project in light of contemporary processes of globalization, particularly in a country like the United States, where death and war are sanitized by the media in neatly packaged soundbites and high-tech images; so that the actual effects of U.S. bombing campaigns on a variety of regions have been depicted mainly through the eyes of the missiles that were launched. The systemic nature of media-driven spectacle desensitizes viewers and leads to the possibility of even the most thoughtful representations of oppression being interpreted as yet another spectacle.

The politics of representation is complicated because there is no objective, measurable distinction between voyeurism and witnessing; the distinction is qualitative and subtle. This is further complicated by the effects of globalization since our creations may travel rapidly across national borders and have different meanings for audiences in different locations. Moreover, given the market-driven nature of the global economy, our acts of representation are continually turned into commodities while individual writers and activists have little control over the ways in which their work will be interpreted and used. The distinction between witnessing and voyeurism can be seen most easily in examples from the mainstream media. For example, the twenty-four-hour cable news networks explicitly nurture voyeurism when they endlessly harness stories of personal crises, violence and loss. Yet the line between voyeurism and witnessing is complicated because it also depends on the reaction of the individual watching—a reaction not necessarily in emotional terms, but in terms of how the viewer acts in response. There is, for example, a clear difference between someone who watches images of violence and oppression and then simply switches off the television and someone whose conscience is sparked enough to assume a sense of responsibility for what she has witnessed. The distinction is a subtle one, and, ultimately, one in which only a honest self-examination can determine. Such distinctions are subtle because they rest on the usually invisible question of spiritual responsibility.

WITNESSING AND SPIRITUAL RESPONSIBILITY

If witnessing must rest on a deep sense of ethical responsibility, it also brings with it a spiritual responsibility. It is here that witnessing can become an active and potentially transformative practice, through a move that reconnects the notion of the witness to its sacred meaning. There can be no more sacred endeavor than to see, to understand, the injustices inflicted on individuals and social groups—that is, to bear witness to the suffering of others. For example, many Jewish individuals have spoken and written about the sacredness of the memory of the Holocaust.[17] This consciousness of the sacredness of their suffering, survival and memory can help us to understand in deeper ways the question of what it means to witness and remember suffering. Bearing witness to suffering of any kind is a sacred project because of the spiritual responsibility it places on the witness. But what does it mean to speak of spiritual responsibility in this way, and why spiritual responsibility rather than, say, political responsibility? To witness suffering—whether this suffering stems from physical, emotional or psychic violence, or from severe material deprivation—I have come to believe, is to witness a part of the deepest unfolding of the soul. It is to witness the unimaginable horrors that human beings are capable of inflicting on each other, in which many of us are implicated; it is to witness the ways in which these horrors pierce through the very being of another individual or group of people. It is to witness the kinds of acts and behaviors that, for centuries, philosophers have struggled to come to terms with and have tried unsuccessfully to make sense of through the safety of bounded rationality. It is a process in which the suffering of others sparks the soul of the witness, who may either accept the challenge of understanding and responsibility, or who may instead curtail the spiritual possibilities by refusing to see or by seeing voyeuristically. Such an act of witnessing, by definition, implicates the observer; there is no such thing as a detached observer if detached means separate, unconnected or without responsibility. It is the choice of the witness that determines whether the act of witnessing will become transformative or not; that is, transformative for the witness and, in the witness' acceptance of a deeper sense of social and spiritual responsibility, transformative in a larger sense as well. Witnessing the suffering of others can open the soul to the rigors of spiritual principles such as compassion, love and justice; rigors that are far more demanding in terms of spiritual responsibility than any of the ethical principles I have discussed.

What then makes the act of witnessing transformative in a practical sense? There is no single or uniform answer to this query. In some instances it may involve the witness intervening in some way in an incident that is unfolding; there are many everyday examples of witnessing acts of violence that may spur action, even if such action is as simple as providing material means to someone less-privileged whom we may pass by in the street. It is easy to forget the dailiness of witnessing that each of us engages in. But the transformative potential of witnessing does not always involve action in the immediate situation at hand. This is a break from the more conventional assumptions usually made by progressive activists and intellectuals about what their responsibility is when they encounter wrongs. As we have seen, for instance, a researcher may witness hidden experiences of suffering in which she is bound *not* to intervene in order not to cause harm to the individual or group in question. For example, a woman may reveal an experience of sexual harassment in her workplace under strict conditions of confidentiality; in such a case, revealing or attempting to correct the situation may not only violate this confidentiality but may cause further harm by jeopardizing the woman's only means of economic support or causing severe social ostracism from the woman's community. What can make this act of witnessing transformative, then, is neither conventional political or social acts of intervention nor the sort of technical experimentations with new textual strategies of writing and representation, but instead, a spiritualization of the suffering being witnessed.

Such a process enables the spiritual learning of the witness, and it is for this reason that the act of witnessing represents an immediate space of potential transformation for the observer. Most traditional intellectuals who have unknowingly acted as witnesses in their research have not understood the significance of the spiritual dimension of their knowledge practices. Instead they have ignored or underplayed this dimension of self-learning and assumed at worst that their subjects are simply passive objects of study or at best the means through which to teach others. This process of self-learning should not be mistaken for a narcissistic confessional of privilege or of an exploitative relationship where the subjects being witnessed provide the fodder for the benefit of the more privileged observer. Nor should it be assumed that the witness can use empathy to "know" the suffering of others. To speak of witnessing as a basis for gaining spiritual knowledge is to humble the witness in ways that are currently unimaginable in traditional academic institutions. For it suggests a frightening possibility that those of us who claim to be the knowers are in fact the ones being taught. Since traditional intellectuals place tremendous stake in the power and control that comes from studying and observing others, it is perhaps not surprising that such possibilities have been placed outside the secure fences of our bounded rationalities. But it is this understanding of the spiritual meaning of witnessing that teaching, writing or other forms of social activism must engage with. Such actions involve a kind of giving away or giving back of the immense learning which the witness has received. This is, of course, a significant reversal of current practices of knowledge production, which assume that we own that which we witness. This assumed ownership is linked to and has been exacerbated by capitalism, which treats knowledge as property, but it is not only reducible to such economic processes; commodified knowledge is simply a material manifestation of our own attitudes and behaviors and such commodification could be undone in an instant if we could learn to enact in new ways the original, sacred meaning of witnessing.

KNOWLEDGE AND NON-VIOLENCE

Witnessing and the actions that stem from it enable a spiritualization of the suffering of the individual or group in question; and, as I have argued in the previous chapter, this spiritualization of suffering is a fundamental dimension of the practice of non-violent transformation. The knowledge practices used to represent suffering, which I have been discussing, are thus simply one dimension of a broader expanse of non-violent transformative practice. This is, in effect, an endeavor to extend the idea of redemptive suffering so that the knowledge of suffering can also become redemptive. This should not be seen as an abstract or otherworldly philosophical reflection on knowledge, for it rests squarely on the need for ongoing, practical action in our approaches, attitudes and practices of knowledge production. Imagine for a moment the possibility of applying the principles of non-violence to our knowledge practices. Critics like Gayatri Spivak have rightly called our attention to the kinds of epistemic violence which knowledge has produced through history. But a spiritualized perspective suggests that not only can we move beyond a paralyzing recognition of the violence of knowledge but also that it is possible to engage in non-violent knowledge practices (of writing, teaching and learning) that lead to the kind of transformative knowledge that contemporary intellectuals and activists desire.

What might it mean, then, to work towards a non-violent practice of knowledge? In many ways this simply takes us back to the general reflections on non-violent practice in the preceding chapter; it is for this very reason that I have said that the current debates on theory and practice in Women's Studies are misguided when they make false separations between knowledge and practice. I have, for instance, already touched on some of the ethical considerations that arise in the process of research as well as on the proposition that a cornerstone of any transformative form of knowledge must rest on non-violent principles. But, as we have seen, the practice of non-violence is about much more than not causing physical injury towards another. Developing a non-violent approach to knowledge is further complicated in a world in which knowledge has been structured by institutional systems of economic, political and cultural power. The task of engaging in non-violent knowledge practices cannot be reduced to a simple set of curriculum or methodological guidelines; what it requires is an approach which infuses the entire process of research, writing, teaching and learning with the philosophy and principles of non-violence.

Consider for instance the question of teaching. The dynamics in classrooms and universities are often far from any practice of non-violence. This is of course in many ways peculiar to education in the United States, where freedom of the mind has been oddly subverted into a kind of disrespect for learning, disrespect which I have unfortunately noticed tends to be especially evident in more "progressive" classes and sites of learning, such as Women's Studies. This is particularly the case where teaching requires that students examine their own locations and relations to larger structures of international economic, gendered and racial structures of inequality—students' resistance to such examinations often leads them to react with anger. Moreover I have found that more often than not students are likely to attack each other in harsh ways. Over the years I have often watched groups of students ostracize individual students whose views they may not agree with, even as they have spoken the language of universal sisterhood. Such small daily examples of disrespect, I am suggesting, are not just random incidents but are examples of attitudes and behaviors that violate the principles of a non-violent approach to knowledge practices. I point to them not to suggest that students as a group are essentially difficult but because such every-day acts point to a deeper process. Nor are such instances of everyday violence limited to students; such dynamics characterize relations between colleagues both in academic and non-academic workplaces, and are shaped by the social identities of individuals. I focus on students because those of us with the authority to teach have a particular respon-sibility to students. The acts which I have described represent a kind of spiritual blockage to learning and self-examination which ultimately prevents the kind of real social change which feminism is concerned with. I have come to believe that, as teachers, we have a responsibility to help students think about the dailiness of violent and non-violent prac-tice, particularly in situations where we are addressing questions of social change. For if we cannot even work from a place of humility when we are in a privileged site of learning, why expect the world out there to change?

To speak of teaching as a dimension of the practice of non-violent knowledge in this way is not the same as some feminist approaches to pedagogy which attempt to become democratic by dismantling structures of authority in the classroom.[18] Constructively negotiating power relations in the classroom is not the same as assuming that authority is not necessary. This dismissal of authority also sometimes operates with a related belief that feminist classrooms should be a comforting "safe space." Thinking of a non-violent form of practice in the classroom, however, has little to do with getting rid of authority; furthermore, the practice of non-violence is anything but safe or comfortable for, as we have seen, it demands an unrelenting embrace of risk and critical self-evaluation. I single out the Women's Studies classroom as an example not to engage in the misplaced Women's Studies-bashing which is often a favorite political trend in the public sphere but because, like many other progressive interdisciplinary fields of knowledge, it has so much potential. Students in these programs consciously enter the classroom because they are committed to creating a different kind of world.

If the knowledge practices of those who are most committed to social transformation cannot confront and break out of such lived enactments of epistemic violence, what changes can we possibly expect to be made in more conservative academic sites? The point I am addressing is in fact a complete reversal of the way in which the theory-practice dichotomy is framed. The question that is usually asked is, What use is this knowledge, this theory, to the world if it does not have immediately apparent, visible effects on the rest of the world, i.e., what is the use of knowledge if it is not practical? What I am asking is, What is the use of espousing practice if it is not even possible to behave in transformative ways in the very privileged, comfortable space of the classroom of an American university?

I began this discussion of the possibilities of non-violent knowledge with an examination of the responsibilities of students in order to underline once again the dailiness of transformative practice. If we focus exclusively on the larger national and global structures of power that currently shape "knowledge," we risk too easily displacing the significance of individual social responsibility. By this I do not mean the kind of personal responsibility which evades relationships of power, as conservative ideologies which focus on individual responsibility usually do. Rather, the point is to focus on the everyday ways in which, as individuals, we are often implicated in the very things we seek to change and transform. The dailiness of harmful knowledge practices is much more prevalent than some might think. In many ways higher education in the United States rests on a confusion between intellectual rigor and academic standards on the one hand, and abusive approaches to teaching and learning on the other. Educational institutions of all levels and across nations routinely enact a form of psychic violence against students. Over the years I have heard countless revelations from students of such violence; educational institutions can serve as sites for the reproduction of racial, gender and class hierarchies in deeply personal and injurious ways. From a spiritualized, non-violent perspective, knowledge that is based on such practices of harm can never be transformative. Such local practices are in fact simply a microcosm of the larger global structures of power where knowledge is commodified in order to serve the economic interests of dominant groups, and where knowledge practices routinely rest on a relationship of exploitative extraction from less-privileged groups. For instance, multinational corporations, usually from the advanced industrialized countries, are currently engaged in routine thefts of the indigenous knowledge of local communities in mostly "Third World" contexts through international systems of patenting and marketing.[19]

Such acts of theft represent a stark manifestation of a mistaken view of knowledge as property; they are thus blatant violations of a spiritualized non-violent approach to knowledge. Yet anyone who views knowledge as a commodity that can or must be stolen is in fact acting with a profound ignorance of the meaning of knowledge. At the deepest level, a spiritualized non-violent approach to knowledge is not just a negative approach, that is, it is not just about ensuring that our knowledge practices don't harm others. Rather, such an approach is grounded on a more intimate understanding of the meaning of boundless nature of universal knowledge.

UNIVERSAL KNOWLEDGE AS WISDOM AND MYSTERY

In the academy, there are few things more controversial than to make a claim about knowledge or truth as universal. Feminist and post-modern insights have now well demonstrated that throughout history the truths that have been named as universal are in fact partial at best and distorted at worst. For example, this distortion has taken the form of partial forms of knowledge derived from European contexts being cast as universal principles, such as reason, freedom and knowledge.[20] Such distortions have understandably led to a discomfort with claims to universality. The error in this discomfort is that such distortions are confused with universality itself. Universal principles do exist; the problem is not with the idea of universal principles, but with the fact that these principles have been distorted and misapplied, and that the narrow, partial material world views of some cultures have paraded as universal truths.

The universality of knowledge has, in our recent history, been mistaken for the colonizing desire to generalize and to establish sameness and uniformity between all peoples and cultures. In fact, the universal nature of knowledge rests on the infinite depth of wisdom; it represents, so to speak, the wisdom of the universe. The boundlessness of such wisdom is very different from the contemporary beliefs of many traditional intellectuals, which assume that knowledge is like a pie or a piece of territory that has to be carved up, so that if one individual gains a large piece there will be less for the rest of us. This assumption of scarcity is of course a prevalent assumption in current free-market economic theories and models, but it is tragic when it becomes the foundational assumption that defines learning and teaching. Gaining wisdom, in fact, represents the spiritual learning that we engage in throughout our lives; it has nothing to do with the credentials we acquire or with assumptions of intellectual superiority. This distinction between wisdom and knowledge has not even begun to be recognized by traditional intellectuals;[21] and for those progressive intellectuals who speak and dream of social change, such a recognition is of fundamental importance. As Bede Griffiths put it,

> If mankind is to survive—and it is his survival which is now threatened—it can only be through a change of heart, a metanoia, which will make science subordinate to wisdom. The discursive reason which seeks to dominate the world and imprisons man in the narrow world of the conscious mind must be dethroned, and must acknowledge its dependence on the transcendent Mystery, which is beyond rational consciousness. (19)

Imagine, for instance, if we were to allow our understanding of knowledge to sit within a sense of mystery; this is in many ways unthinkable for even traditional disciplines in the social sciences, let alone the sciences.

Yet it is precisely this sense of mystery, of the unknowable, that has permeated a great deal of recent feminist writing; the partiality of knowledge which feminist thinkers have talked about[22] is not antithetical to universal knowledge, it is intrinsic to it. For this sense of mystery, this sense of transcendent unknowability, is at the heart of understanding the universality of our existence. It is a humbling sense of mystery that can prevent us from turning our own perceptions and experiences into the colonizing will to make others conform to our definitions of life which so many thinkers have criticized; the colonizing impulse that has distorted the meaning of knowledge into a will to conquer. It is a sense of mystery that dispels the mistaken assumption that the intellectual, writer, teacher or activist is the knower rather than a witness who is always in the process of being known.

Such transformative knowledge practices are not only a possibility, they are a necessity in these times. When such possibilities are not opened up, we risk turning into cynics, critics who can only use intellectual weapons to dismantle the mistakes of others without creating paths for a different way of thinking, learning and being. This leads to a kind of alienation of the spirit which is so prevalent amongst academics, often in those who believe or once believed in the possibilities of transformation. My own hope is that such reflections on the possibilities of spiritualized knowledge will contribute in some way to different kinds of feminist knowledge practices inside and outside the academy.

Chapter 5   **Spirituality**

In the world in which we currently live, it is a risky proposition to speak of politics and spirituality in the same breath. More than ever, the politicization of spirituality produces grave consequences through the actions of various religious nationalisms, conservative social ideologies cast in the name of religion, and wars of and against terrorism. It is not surprising that progressive intellectuals and activists adhere more than ever to a secular framework for social justice and political action. Although secularism seems the antithesis of the need for the spiritualization of practice and knowledge which I have been reflecting on, it is not. This is because, in fact, the current debate on secular and religious politics has little to do with the questions of spirituality and social justice that I have been addressing.

Critics of secularism have in most cases focused on the problems with state secularism. These critical responses have taken several forms. The most well-known challenge to secularism has been posed by religious nationalist movements that have focused their energies on attempts to seize state power and redefine it in religious terms. However other, more subtle, criticisms of secularism have also been made. For instance, some postcolonial critics have suggested that secularism is an ideology developed in the West that was imposed on non-Western countries through colonialism. Other critics have argued that secularism has not proved to be an adequate framework for managing religious diversity and preventing religious conflict; for instance, some have suggested that secularism often incorporates elements of the dominant religion in a country and does not in actuality separate religion from the state.[1]

Spiritualized social transformation, unlike existing forms of politicized religion, does not and cannot represent a political struggle against secularism because its goals are not focused on the seizure of political authority and state power. To that extent, it does not represent an attack on state policies of secularism which are designed to preserve religious tolerance and diversity, as well as the freedom *not* to practice or support the beliefs of any organized religion. Secularism is a necessary, practical governmental mechanism for preserving freedom from religious oppression. Yet both the failures of secular states to prevent religious conflict and oppression and the rise of religious nationalism point to the importance of reflecting more deeply on what it means to speak about spirituality at the present time. For simply invoking spirituality as a new metaphor or goal can neither circumvent nor transcend the hazards of power, domination and hierarchy; a language of spirituality is as power-laden as any other traditional "secular" or material language of power. To assume otherwise is to mistake spirituality for an esoteric abstraction devoid of material implications.

There is perhaps no better demonstration of the ways in which spirituality has become circumscribed by social hierarchies and relationships of power than in the institutionalized discourses, practices and organizational mechanisms of the major organized religions. The most visible examples of such hierarchies are the gendered practices and politics which have excluded women from ecclesiastic and priestly functions and reproduced gendered ideas of "purity." In these ideologies, understandings of spiritual purity are projected onto the material bodies of women, for instance through ritual taboos on women's biological functions such as menstruation and pregnancy; such ideologies have also reproduced repressive attitudes towards women's sexuality and towards homosexuality. These social prescriptions, encoded within the institutional practices and textual interpretations of organized religions, have little to do with these religions' deeper mystical truths.[2]

In recent times, a great deal of attention has been paid to the rise of religious fundamentalisms and religious nationalism across the world. Although the national security interests of the United States have skewed this to an almost exclusive focus on Islamic fundamentalism, other forms have also continued to grow,[3] though well beneath the lens of the mainstream media in the United States. While public attention has focused on the more violent manifestations of the politicization of religion, the problem of religious intolerance is deeper and more profound than simply the explicitly chauvinistic or violent versions of religious practice. One of the biggest limitations of organized religion has been the ways in which it has linked spiritual teaching and practice to a process of identification, that is, bounded forms of religious identity. Such a process runs counter to the kind of radical disidentification that, as I have argued in chapter 2, lies at the heart of spiritualized social transformation. The process of identification which most organized religions have enabled, if not actively produced, has prevented a transformation of the hierarchies and divisions that have led to conflict and suffering throughout history. The mystical teachings of such religions speak of love, forgiveness and a form of universal oneness; yet the religious institutions that have taken on the sacred responsibility of interpreting and disseminating these teachings have placed them within rigid structures of identity, carving up the world into autonomous religions. Within the context of these religious structures, their teachings are grounded on an identity-based claim to a monopoly over "Truth," even when their practitioners attempt to promote inter-religious harmony and tolerance. Why then would it be surprising that history has been shaped by what seems to be an eternity of religious conflict, when those who speak on behalf of the sacred have carved up the divine into a series of discrete territories?

Spirituality has literally been treated as a form of territory, which religious institutions and believers have battled over and then guarded access to. The borders of these territories have been not only symbolic but also material. Religious leaders, institutions and, in some instances, states have policed the lines of who is allowed the authority to interpret the divine and have used this authority to sanction and constrain social behavior. Furthermore, these religious representatives have often used such forms of control for material gains, including political and economic power. The convergence of a territorialized divinity with a territorialized nation that we see in contemporary forms of religious nationalism should be of no surprise to anyone. Most critics on the left have spoken of this as an assault on modern values of secularism—that is, the intrusion of religious beliefs in the political realm. Yet what I want to suggest is that the tendency here is not with the religious encroaching on the secular but, to the contrary, the secular encroaching on the sacred. Contemporary hegemonic institutions of organized religion, in their pursuit of state power, are in fact engaging in a kind of secular colonization of the divine. Social transformation thus also requires a form of spiritual revolution that decolonizes the realm of spirituality. In other words, while in previous chapters I have focused primarily on the need to spiritualize existing approaches to social justice and activism in order to rid these approaches of all forms of hierarchy and oppression, in this chapter I am turning to the ways in which spirituality needs to be transformed and freed from these limitations.

DECOLONIZING THE DIVINE

What is at stake when addressing the colonization of the divine are the ways in which the realms of the spiritual and material are demarcated and relinked through the existing dichotomy of the secular and the sacred. Advocates of secularism have proposed models which, while they have varied in different times and places, for the most part have been concerned with the problem of managing the relationship between political and religious authority.[4] Modern political authority is embodied in the state and its loosely affiliated public institutions such as schools and universities. Religious groups that have attacked secularism have been concerned with the question of where the line between these two forms of authority should be drawn. Proponents of politicized religion are invested in struggling against secularism precisely because of their own secular interests in authority and institutional control. The irony is that they are in fact engaged in a struggle to gain access to the secular power of the state. Such movements based on politicized religion treat spirituality as a tool with which to seize state power; they harness divinity in order to gain political authority. This is the meaning of the secular colonization of the divine, which most organized religions are engaged in and which has culminated in extreme forms of modern religious nationalisms and fundamentalisms.

There are numerous examples of the secular colonization of the divine. Religious states that use political power to impose particular interpretations of religion (which are usually socially conservative) certainly abound. Such cases already occupy a central place in the Western imagination, as well as in the Western feminist imagination, due to the repressive gendered ideologies of such regimes.[5] In addition, the racialized and ethnocentric missionary practices that were embedded in European colonial rule in Asia and Africa in the nineteenth and early twentieth century also provide a vivid instance of the historical violence of identity-driven religious activity. These practices are about a secular will to power, derived from the desire for ownership and control. Let us consider two instances from two completely disparate contexts in order to flesh out the subtle ways in which this process of secular colonization of the divine occurs.

In recent times, the violent nature of religious conflict and intolerance has become so brutally apparent across the world that we have seen numerous religious leaders speak of a need for interreligious harmony and a respect for the existence of religious difference. Such developments are of invaluable significance, given the fact that religious leaders of institutionalized faiths continue to have an immense impact on a majority of individuals in the world.[6] Yet the language of religious difference, even when it is framed with a language of anti-colonialism, can be used in ways that engage in the colonizing production of material hierarchies and injustices. For instance, in contemporary India, Hindu nationalists have used the language of anti-colonialism to portray the "foreign" religions of Christianity and Islam[7] as colonizing, invading forces that are a threat to the indigenous religious traditions of India.[8] A presumably anti-colonial endeavor for the preservation of religious difference is depicted, by these nationalists, as a need to preserve what they define as the oppressed religions of Hinduism, Buddhism, Jainism and

Sikhism. At first glance, this may seem to some like an innocuous or even a noble act given the association of Christianity in India with the violence of British rule and the current preoccupation with real and stereotyped threats of violent, militant forms of Islamic fundamentalism. Yet such a framework must be understood in relation to a political situation in which this militant Hindu nationalist movement has grown in strength over the past few decades and has violently targeted minority Muslim and Christian religious communities in India. In this instance, the language of an anti-colonial call for the preservation of religious difference, in fact, masks the perpetuation of deep-rooted inequalities.

While there have been numerous academic and political writings on the negative effects of politicized Hindu nationalism,[9] these writings have overlooked this process of the secular colonization of the divine which is carried out in the name of anti-colonialism. The carving out of Hinduism into a singular political, cultural and religious *identity*-based movement distorts the mystical teachings of Hinduism, teachings which can provide many of the foundations for a radical, egalitarian form of social transformation based on a disidentified notion of the Self. The identity-based movement of politicized Hinduism has perpetuated secular material projects that range from changing and distorting the writing of history to the destruction of mosques (as with the destruction of the Babri Masjid and the movement to build a Hindu temple in its place at Ayodhya) to the scapegoating of Muslim and Christian communities. Such processes are then, unfortunately, inadvertently reproduced in countries like the United States when scholars and teachers of religions classify Indian religions (or "Indic traditions," which is the academic term) to include Hinduism, Buddhism, Jainism and Sikhism but not Islam or Christianity. Thus the territorialization of spirituality through the hegemonic boundaries of political nationalism is safely guarded in what is usually a well-intentioned project of teaching about religious and cultural difference. This is simply one example that I set forth to demonstrate the way our educational practices subscribe to and reinforce social hierarchies and participate in this process of colonization in subtle ways.

The irony is that most people, including both proponents *and* critics of this particular form of religious nationalism, view it as an attack on secularism. On the contrary, what I have described is a prime example of an attack on the divine, for it represents an attempt to secularize faith and spirituality, not an attempt to spiritualize the material world. This is one of the most important issues that must be recognized in any process of comprehensive social transformation. To secularize spirituality is to harness divine beliefs, faiths, truths and the deepest sources of wisdom in order to pursue secular, material ends—whether such ends are about winning elections or gaining economic, political or cultural power for a particular community. To spiritualize the material realm, on the other hand, is to engage in the non-violent practices that transform individual, community and national attachments away from vested interests in bounded forms of power and control. It is in this sense that I have spoken of the impossibility of separating the spiritual and material realms. And it is in this sense that I have suggested that such a convergence of the spiritual and material, while it may challenge many aspects of a secular belief system, is not an attack on state secularism, when secularism represents a governing mechanism designed to protect against oppression by dominant and hierarchical religious institutions and communities.

I have used the example of politicized Hinduism in India because it is one which I am familiar with. But these dynamics are not limited to religious nationalism in India. For example, the fact that in countries such as India, Christianity is viewed as a "Western" religion is a historical and spiritual distortion that stems from a legacy of empire and colonialism—not only the more recent empires of nineteenth-century Europe but also the more distant legacy of the Roman Empire. Christianity, as an organized religion, is a material product of empire which has, in many ways, little to do with the actual teachings and practices of Christ, who was manifested as a Jew living in Palestine. If anything, Jesus' teachings are the essence of a radical mystical revolutionary aimed at decolonizing the divine from all forms of hierarchy, control and injustice. This is what mystic and writer Andrew Harvey, in seeking an answer to the question, "Why did the Roman authorities perceive Jesus as a threat when he preached and lived non-violence?" explains,

> The deepest answer is that, taken together, Jesus' teachings challenged the entire patriarchal order on which Roman power was based. To a world obsessed by power, Jesus offered

a vision of the radiance of the powerlessness and powerful vulnerability of love; to a culture riddled with authoritarianism of every kind, he gave a vision of the holiness of inner and outer poverty and a critique of the vanity and horror of all forms of worldly achievement; to a society arranged at every level into different hierarchies, he presented in his own life, being, and daily practice a vision of a radical and all embracing egalitarianism designed to end forever those dogmas and institutions that keep women enslaved, races separated from each other, the poor starving, and the rich rotting in prisons of selfish luxury.[10]

It is this contestation of all forms of hierarchy and repression, this reversal of empire, that is the heart of the practice of a spiritualized process of social transformation, and that threatens all investments of power in both the secular and religious worlds. However, this process of transformation was particularly potent in Jesus' time because it simultaneously revolutionized both the social and spiritual orders of the time. Truth was, in a sense, being taken back from both the Roman and the religious authorities, not in order to form a new religion, but as a process of reclaiming spirituality from the hierarchies and dogmas that sought to tame it.

One of the spiritual errors made throughout history is the claim, made across religious traditions, to a monopoly on the truth. This claim is both material and secular. For to claim such a monopoly is to assume that truth can be owned—demarcated, patented and then marketed to the rest of the world—by a single religious institution, hierarchy or organization. Such an assumption is completely contrary to the mystical teachings of the very institutionalized religions that operate with it. To dispel the assumption that truth can be owned is not to revert back to the postmodern misunderstanding that truth does not exist or can never be known. It is to begin to decolonize the divine—truth, spirit, faith, understanding, knowledge, wisdom—from the material colonization which religious institutions, with their secular interests, have been engaged in for centuries. Let us consider then some of the spiritual directions that this process of decolonization can lead to.

SPIRITUALITY AND SOCIAL RESPONSIBILITY

I have been arguing throughout this book that lasting transformation requires nothing less than a complete transformation of the ways in which the material and spiritual realms are currently partitioned off and then reconnected in ways that produce deep-seated social hierarchies within and between nations. Such an approach points to a kind of spirituality that fully embraces social responsibility. It requires an understanding of spirituality that is linked to a continual process of learning and understanding the world as well as the historical and contemporary roots of social injustice. Too often, spiritual practice has been thought of as a purely private endeavor,[11] whether this privacy has been defined in terms of an individual, family or community practice. But in the kind of globalized world in which we live, a decolonization of the divine necessitates a spiritual practice that includes a willingness to confront all forms of political and socioeconomic injustice, an approach which must be engaged in without reverting to the colonizing forms of missionary-based attitudes to social change that have shaped both secular and religious movements.

Without an understanding of how to manifest one's own spiritual work and practice in the world, global material-spiritual transformation will not be possible. Spiritual practice that is based on a belief in a separation between the spiritual and the material is at best a form of escapism and at worst a means for the perpetuation of deep-seated forms of injustice. It pervades some "New Age" versions of spirituality in the United States as well as many Western adaptations of so-called "Eastern" religions. The result is a form of commodified spirituality that is dislocated from an understanding of global historical, social and economic inequalities and that often reproduces orientalist images of an essentially spiritual "East." India, for instance, is stereotypically depicted as a land of spirituality—a pure source that can provide the cure for the cultural and spiritual alienation of the "West" without any need for an understanding of the historical, political and economic context of such spiritual traditions. Yet this is not just about a question of stereotypes—of India as the timeless land of gurus, yogis and ashrams with the means to eternal bliss. The problem is that such an approach is based on a form of spiritual appropriation that is devoid of social responsibility.

By casting places like India or Tibet as places of pure spirituality, individuals who seek fulfillment or learning, either by travelling to ashrams or by learning from Western gurus who have studied with an "authentic" "Eastern" teacher, do not have to take on a spiritual responsibility for the social injustices and global political and economic relations of inequality that disrupt easy dichotomies between "East" and "West." Without such responsibility, there is a serious risk of spirituality being transformed into yet another consumption practice for one's own personal well-being and comfort, another commodity that is meant to alleviate the stresses of living without the discomfort of challenging any of the structures of power that shape the world. This commodification is already evident in the product-oriented quality of some of the centers dealing with spirituality in the United States. But it is by no means limited to the United States.[12] For example, even India is now characterized by a growing industry of "New Age" therapies for physical, spiritual and emotional healing and transformation, an industry that primarily caters to the urban and upper-middle classes that can afford the steep fees that practitioners charge.[13]

The problem is not with the intentions of the individuals seeking meaning through such practices. Many so-called "New Age" therapies often do help their seekers in certain ways and draw on important kinds of spiritual principles that can point to healthier ways of living and being. Blanket dismissals of alternative forms of therapies and spiritual practices often stem from a fear or sense of condescension on the part of individuals with secular or more traditional religious beliefs.[14] But where the alternative practices of both "New Age" seekers and Western spiritual seekers "looking East" for salvation falter is on the question of power—for there is a disturbing lack of recognition of the ways in which power permeates social relations, including those social relations within spiritual realms. For example, spiritual seekers in the United States are often drawn to spiritual elements and rituals of religious traditions such as Hinduism or Buddhism, yet they do not usually define spiritual development as including a sense of responsibility to questions of political, social and economic justice in the lands from which they seek salvation. For instance, Western believers in Hinduism often do not feel a sense of responsibility to address the implications for India of a militant politicized Hindu nationalism. Spirituality is mistaken for a kind of privatized safe space that should not be contaminated by the muddy realms of politics and power. Yet it is precisely this assumption that has allowed spirituality to become hijacked by conservative, repressive movements across the world. This is all too evident in the current rise of fundamentalist forms of Islam, although it is mistakenly being assumed by the Western public (although not only the Western public) that this distortion of spirituality into acts of terrorism is somehow peculiar to Islamic militants.[15] However, history shows all too clearly that this distortion is a much more universal act. It is the same resort to terrorism when Hindu militants tear down mosques and Christian militants bomb abortion clinics. It is true that these acts, which occur within the boundaries of nation-states, do not spark the global instability of acts of terrorism across nation-states; but they are acts of terrorism nevertheless.

In the U.S., any form of spirituality that cannot confront the United States' hegemonic political, military, cultural and economic global becomes a mask for the power and privilege that stems from residing in the heart of empire. It leads to a kind of spirituality which, in imperceivable ways, becomes rooted in the bounded identity of national security.[16] For example, any form of spirituality which accepts the assumption that terrorism can be defined as that which threatens oneself and not "the other" will remain embedded in global relationships of power and domination. Forms of spirituality that do not include a confrontation with the terrors of poverty, social justice and the violence caused by American political and economic might—even while they might provide some forms of healing and growth—cannot in the long run provide the kind

of transformation which the world as a whole and each of us as individuals needs. Consider, for instance, how this curtailment of spiritual growth unfolded in the immediate aftermath of the 9/11 terrorist attacks. In the days following the attacks, the mainstream American public became infused with questions of faith, God and spirituality. Media reports described a new surge of spiritual interest as people, long used to a basic form of national comfort and security not present in most of the world, struggled to cope with the deeper meaning behind the loss and fear which was suddenly thrust on them. Some religious leaders and media reporters even went as far as to describe this as a form of spiritual renewal that had emerged from the ravages of the World Trade Center buildings. Yet it only took a few months for the general public to become engulfed in military campaigns, racial profiling and the disbursal of million dollar victims' funds. This is not to say that there may not have been any spiritual transformations among individuals;[17] but the claim of national spiritual renewal had turned once again into a politics of fear and retribution.

Such dynamics can easily be interpreted in conventional political analyses of strategic defense, nationalism and political behavior and attitudes. Yet the questions that linger concern the spiritual meaning of such dynamics. Where did the reported spiritual renewal go? Did it simply revert to privatized spirituality as individuals coped with personal grief and loss? Is it manifested in everyday acts, as some people try to make constructive changes in their dealings with their families and communities? Both of these avenues are likely possibilities. However there is, I believe, a third, more serious dimension to this question—that is, the ways in which the spiritual meaning of the terrorist attacks was impeded by the material structures of race and nation. For ultimately, at a national level, the spiritual self-examination which was momentarily spurred by the horror of the terrorist attacks could not transcend such structures. In the months after the attacks, individuals and leaders from other countries, while sympathizing with the grief of Americans, began to voice the frustration captured in the statement, "Americans do not have a monopoly on grief and suffering." This frustration stems from the single-minded American focus on its own policy interests, and its subordination of other forms of conflict and oppression in relation to these interests.[18] Yet at another level, this frustration cannot be viewed merely in terms of state policy, for examples of this presumed monopoly on grief can also be seen on mainstream television networks and in public discourse.[19] These points are not made to support a knee-jerk anti-American sentiment, nor to devalue the very real grief and fear of many Americans, nor to justify acts of violent terrorism. What these points elucidate is an inability of the mainstream American public to use its own grief and suffering to connect to the underlying causes of conflict and the sources of suffering which most of the world experiences in a frighteningly normalized fashion. This kind of American exceptionalism in the realm of suffering assumes that the value of life lost is rendered unique by virtue of citizenship.

I have argued in chapter 3 that activists such as Gandhi and Martin Luther King, Jr., presented deep insights into the redemptive potential of suffering. However, turning suffering into a creative, redemptive and ultimately transformative force is not an inevitable process. Existing conflicts of violence and retribution, such as the Israeli-Palestinian conflict or other numerous longstanding historical cycles of violence based on religion or ethnicity, provide devastating evidence of this fact. When the spiritual meaning of suffering is bound by the material structures of race, community or nation, the transformative possibilities of suffering are aborted and usually lead instead to longstanding historical cycles of retribution in the name of justice. It is this kind of retributive justice which the United States finds itself steeped in, backed by the power of empire. It is this kind of retributive justice which forecloses the spiritualization of suffering.

This contradictory position, where the most powerful nation in the world views itself as a victim under attack, now proves to be one of the most challenging contexts in which to live for any individual committed to a spiritual transformation of the self and world. The current climate in the U.S. is one which is characterized by a philosophy of "any means necessary" to defend itself against real or perceived threats. Yet it is precisely at the moment of the greatest threat to one's material security that a spiritualized practice of non-violent transformation is most acutely needed, for this question of security poses a spiritual challenge to individuals, communities and nations. As I have argued in previous chapters, from a spiritual perspective, any act that causes harm to another can never ultimately be an act of self-preservation. The preservation of self and security can never be founded on a conflict-oriented model of life. Nor can fences of barbed wire, fearsome military weapons and elaborate methods of surveillance provide security. It is a vivid spiritual lesson to watch the United States, with its sophisticated technologies, military might and economic prosperity, lost in a tidal wave of fear and paranoia, desperately grasping for the new means, the new might, to regain its sense of security. In fact each act of racial profiling, each move towards military expansion, each step towards an offensive movement in the name of victimization leads to a growing loss of spirit and, with it, a growing loss of security. The irony of course is that the American nation unravels[20] in this fashion believing that it alone represents Truth, Justice and Liberty for all; in short, that it alone has God on its side. This story of the slow descent of the United States is simply a metaphor for history. It is a story that has been repeated in different ways in the rise and fall of empires throughout time. The point, then, is not to view this again as an American phenomenon, thereby falling once more into a trap of American exceptionalism. To fail to understand this is to miss the spiritual lessons of history and to be condemned, consequently, to repeat the errors of history.

Social activists and teachers supporting potentially transformative movements (including feminism) can benefit by explicitly confronting these spiritual lessons. But what exactly does this mean? What should or would spirituality mean for social activists and intellectuals? There is of course no single answer to this question. The precise form of one's own spiritual practice is a personal matter—personal, but not private, as spirituality in its essence defines one's relationship with one's self and with the world. I have already spoken, throughout this book, of some of the general spiritual principles that I believe are fundamental for a process of social transformation. But this exploration is in no sense exhaustive; the ways in which such general principles are manifested for each individual will vary in infinite ways that are contingent on one's personal circumstances, history, culture and way of being. In many instances, such a process can involve a return to the mystical roots of the religious tradition of one's own cultural background. However, this is not necessarily the case. Nor is it the case that existing religious traditions are the sole paths of spirituality. Such an assumption rests on a confusion between theology and spirituality. Religious texts and their theological interpreters can provide important sources of learning as long as it is understood that such sources are social products of specific historical circumstances. As is often the case, historical memory of this sort can be both an essential foundation and a lethal obstacle to truth. Often the recovery of the mystical truths embedded in such texts require radical reinterpretations in order to transcend the social codes and constraints that such contextual circumstances produced. And more often than not, the traditional theologians and religious experts are not the ones who can take the risks necessary for such a process of mystical recovery.

LIVED DIVINITY:
Beyond the Commodification of "God"

What I have come to believe is that spirituality—living within and learning about the divine—is very different from theological and religious expertise. It is, after all, much easier to speak for and in the name of God than to struggle to practice a lived spirituality. Imagine for instance how the current fear-based approach to terrorism in the United States might change if the conservative Christian organizations that attack state secularism in the United States for not allowing the ten commandments to be posted in schools would instead attempt to live and teach Christ's life of non-violence. One of the greatest ironies of fundamentalist as well as mainstream organized Christianity[21] has been its inability to understand that the essence of Jesus' divinity lay in a simultaneous rejection of the blame of morality and an unfettered embrace of a lived divinity that is threatening to any form of hierarchy, social exclusion and injustice.

Lived divinity, which is embedded in the mystical roots of organized religion, has nothing to do with the commodification of "God," a particular example of the spiritual commodification I have discussed earlier. It might appear strange to speak of God as a commodity, but that is precisely the way that existing structures of power have demarcated and packaged up the divine. This kind of commodification of the divine can be seen in disparate instances. One sees it in the numerous ways in which false gurus, preachers and even psychics use spirituality to gain wealth and power, resulting in scandals of corruption, theft and abuse. One sees it in the strategies that Hindu nationalists in India used in their campaign to destroy the Babri Masjid mosque and build a Hindu temple in its place. Thomas Hansen describes the local strategies of Hindu organizations such as the Viswa Hindu Parishad (the World Hindu Council) in which activists would take premanufactured bricks to villages as symbolic elements of the temple to be built; local village leaders would "divinize" them in brick consecration ceremonies and then transport them to the site of the mosque.[22] This is a vivid illustration of the commodification of the divine—the sacred was literally packaged into premanufactured bricks and used to build a foundation of violence and hatred.

Yet this example is far from unique. History is replete with instances of politicians and leaders engaging in various forms of violence and war in the name of God. Such invocations of God on behalf of material interests represent the deepest possible form of spiritual commodification. For, in such cases, the divine is turned into a commodified resource which is used to justify and escape responsibility for the consequences of one's actions. It is quite startling to consider the ways in which conceptions of God have been shaped by contemporary definitions of property ownership so that particular individuals, communities and nations actually believe that God could only be on their side, that God is, in effect, theirs to own. It is as if we believe that we can somehow place God in a leash and train him (it is usually a him) to protect our interests, and our interests alone.

What is needed then, for transformation, is simply a radical form of liberation of the divine—within ourselves, our communities, our world. Without this spiritual liberation, enduring social transformation is not possible and movements for social justice will continue to be trapped in cycles of hope and decline, as they have been throughout history. It is precisely this kind of liberation which is needed if the tremendous transformative power of spirituality is not to be continually colonized by such structures of inequality and the social groups that mistakenly believe they benefit from them. Such colonization is a form of spiritual extraction that accompanies the economic extraction from the poor and working classes of marginalized communities across the globe. In other words, the kinds of social and economic exploitation which social activists/thinkers have struggled with for so long do not simply lead to material deprivation, they can also lead to a form of spiritual deprivation—a sense of hopelessness and futility in imagining that a different kind of future is possible.[23] It is the kind of paralysis I have pointed to within the classroom and that exists when individuals feel helpless in changing larger systems or stopping global wars.

As social activists and teachers, we sometimes valorize resistance and, in doing so, risk evading this sense of hopelessness. To do so is both to miss an important place where work needs to be done and to overlook the spiritual strength which subordinated individuals and groups have displayed when they have persisted with visions of transformation in the face of tremendous obstacles. Spiritual learning in this sense is not necessarily to be gained from simply reading religious texts, it is to be gained from those who are subordinated and oppressed. This is the kind of concept which activists drawing on liberation theology put into practice when they spoke of spirituality being located in the poor. The lesson was not that the poor were an idealized embodiment of virtue, but that their struggles for survival and transformation provided them with a form of spiritual wisdom which more privileged individuals needed to learn from. It should not be surprising, then, that some of the deepest spiritual insights have come from the poor and activists working with the poor—indigenous peoples struggling against environmental destruction and genocide, women of color in the U.S. and internationally and from those who have struggled with these marginalized groups. Spirituality in this sense cannot be reduced to a cultural language that one strategically deploys in order to facilitate cross-cultural alliances or to appeal to "other" women and men who appear different from "us."

But what then is the precise model or form which spirituality must take? While I have talked about some of the processes and principles involved, I have not specified a closed definition, as I believe that there is no single answer to this question—to suggest otherwise is to mistake spiritual learning for ownership or missionary activity. I can only reflect on what it has come to mean for me. What spirituality now means to me is a direct, unmediated, ongoing and always-changing relationship with the divine. It is a process in which all dichotomies and distinctions begin to break down so that there is no separation between self and world, between the majestic, unknowable transcendence of the divine beyond and the silent, powerful immanence of the divine within, between a moment and eternity. It is a process which brings one face to face with the boundedness of time, space and history. It is a process that demands an unimaginable intensity of labor in an endeavor which will always seem unfinished. It is a journey that alternates by moment between the magical and the mundane. It is everything that mystics of all of the varied religious and spiritual traditions across time and culture have struggled to describe; yet it is always more than the sum of this everything. It is the essence of the unrepresentable, which Western postmodern intellectuals have been paralyzed by only because they have mistaken the unrepresentable for the unrealizable. It is the only form of power, that lived divinity, that can transform and transcend all forms of hierarchy, injustice and repression. This is the essence of any social or political activism that wants to transform rather than simply resist. Life and history are replete with instances of resistance—small and large. It is transformation that demands the tireless, unending labor of the soul. This has come to represent for me the spiritual-material transformation that can take us to the kind of mystical revolution which is so desperately needed at this moment in history. It is in fact that realizable "utopia" that activists and theorists have yearned for through the centuries. It is, then, both the means and the end for the kind of radical social transformation which I have been reflecting on throughout this book.

Chapter 6   Postscript

Writing about the possibilities of non-violent transformation at the current moment may appear paradoxical given the prevalence of global violence and war and the shift of the current U.S. government towards a policy of overt imperial military expansion. At the time I am writing this, the three-week U.S.-led military campaign against Iraq is being touted as clear proof of the superiority of massive military strength. A spiritualized perspective can enable us to see the fragile and temporary nature of empire, even one as powerful as the current U.S.-led world order. Moments of crisis can be opportunities for real and lasting change and transformation if we understand the significance of such crises and take the risk of acting on such understanding. This is true at the smallest level of everyday personal life, and in the largest sense of global change. Glimpses of this have already been seen in the ways in which hundreds of thousands of people across the world protested in non-violent ways in an attempt to prevent the U.S. war on Iraq. To assess the implications of such movements in terms of the failure to prevent the war is to miss the deeper spiritual significance of such acts. For from a spiritualized perspective, transformation occurs through the practice itself rather than in the visible or material outcome of the practice. This spiritualized understanding of transformation makes our task both more hopeful and more overwhelming. More hopeful because it frees us from narrow definitions of success and failure that are a source of weariness, particularly when struggles are against what appear to be unshakable or immense structures of domination. More overwhelming because it demands a kind of practice that reaches from the smallest, most hidden aspects of our selves and lives to the most visible systemic questions of power and inequality.

The journey of spiritualized transformation is not a journey to sainthood; it has nothing to do with the false grandeur of ideas of spiritual leadership. It is quite simply an ongoing form of spiritual labor that can infuse and radically transform our visions and modes of practice. It is this labor which I have been speaking about when I have suggested throughout this book that utopias are realizable. This suggestion is jarring only when utopia is understood as an idyllic existence, a kind of transcendent heaven free from suffering. In fact, utopia exists at the moment when suffering is transformed into love. Utopia is the labor itself which enables such transformation, not, as is mistakenly assumed, the outcome that results from this labor. Yet it is the unceasing nature of such labor that is most likely to overwhelm, for this kind of spiritualized social activism will often not produce immediate or tangible material results. The spiritual or mystical realms usually make people uneasy precisely because they represent the unseen and, in some ways, the unknown. Such realms run directly counter to the visual technologies and the corresponding fetishization of visibility which have already soaked through the West and have begun to permeate the rest of the world. Given that the world is increasingly driven by the visual media it should not be surprising that even social activists/thinkers usually measure the objectives and successes of social movements in purely visible, material terms. Without realizing it, secular activists/thinkers have come to define social justice in terms of the visible dimensions of human rights—fighting economic poverty, social discrimination, political repression. This is not to say such activity is not of fundamental importance. But when such activities are only assessed in terms of conventional measures, not only does this miss the deeper spiritual significance at hand, it also often leads to a miscalculation of the successes and failures of such activism. The greatest activist works of integrity and honesty often do not produce "successful" outcomes in the conventional material sense of the word. On the other hand, "successful" social movements or activism may often produce their own internal forms of repression, discrimination or exclusion. Yet such contradictions are often not willingly addressed by progressive activist-thinkers. There is, for instance, sometimes a resistance from those who write about the "oppressed" to the possibility of looking at complex inequalities which exist within communities of the marginalized. For privileged individuals committed to social justice, the stakes can sometimes be high in idealizing the poor and oppressed; investing such subaltern groups with an idealized, infallible morality associated with poverty is perhaps the most subtle and most comfortable means of placing such moral (and implicitly spiritual responsibility) on the poor, thus avoiding the responsibility of one's own self-transformation. A spiritualized approach to social justice cannot but confront such contradictions. For the spiritualized practice of non-violence, as we have seen, rests precisely on the strength of the unseen and on an understanding of history which recognizes that centuries are momentary. This is the heart of spiritual revolution.

In this context, the question of gaining immediate results from activism is the least significant of issues at hand. Yet it is precisely this question of immediacy which seems to paralyze many. In discussions of feminism, for instance, I have often gotten the sense that feminism must be about actions that are visible and that can gain visible outcomes — tangible non-governmental organizations, activist and academic conferences, rallies and protests of various kinds form a kind of de facto checklist of what counts as feminist practice. There is almost an unspoken desperation to do something "real" — in the real world, with real women, preferably with the real oppression of the Third World. What occurs in this process is a confusion between the real and the visible. I have come to believe that it is this confusion which is robbing feminism of its spirit and of its potential for transformation. It is this confusion which makes the possibility of social transformation appear overwhelming. In fact, such social transformation is not impossible. It is inevitable. The deepest strength of the spiritual revolutionary stems from a knowledge of this inevitability of social change. To begin to understand this spirit of transformation is to defuse in an instant the paralysis which individuals often feel and to infuse one's practice with an unending sense of renewal.

But what does this mean for the everyday nitty-gritty choices and directions of social activism? What would need to change in the arena of feminist practice? In many cases, there might not be any need for any change at all in the external programs, agendas and objectives of women's organizations or movements. The kind of split between the spiritual and material realms which I have discussed has often not provided a foundation for women's activism. Yet in the United States as well as in traditional secular, modernizing nations in the Third World, indigenous spiritual traditions understandings of women's activism have tended to be simplistically classified as "culture." In the United States, stereotypical views of "Third World" women as victims of patriarchal religious and cultural traditions have more often than not served to foreclose the ways in which women's spiritual expressions and understandings may serve to contest both these patriarchal versions of religion as well as Western definitions of feminism. But the question at hand is more than one of respecting alternative cultural languages of expression for women—indeed, feminism and Women's Studies has often been preoccupied with nothing but the question of respect for cultural difference. The point is that feminist thought and practice in their varied forms have often not considered such expressions as reality—not just the reality or perceived reality of "other women" but a form of universal reality.

This distinction is particularly important because there is already a long orientalist history in which the "East" has been depicted as the quintessential land of spirituality. This dichotomy between a supposedly mystical East and a materialistic West is simply another manifestation of a false separation between the spiritual and the material realms. There is already too long a history of privileged individuals from the West journeying to countries such as India to find a form of individualized spiritual salvation that does not confront issues such as the materiality of poverty or the tragedies of religious violence and oppression. If feminism is to avoid reproducing such colonial legacies it must turn instead to an examination of its own assumptions regarding spirituality. How, for instance, would contemporary feminist theory in the U.S. change if it took seriously the interconnections between the spiritual and material realms in defining its own terms and approaches? How would self-identified feminists act if they viewed themselves as spiritual as well as material and sexual beings? These are questions I have sought to explore throughout this book. However they signify merely a sliver of the concerns and possibilities for social action and thought that could ensue with a spiritualized understanding of movements such as feminism. The reflections in this book represent a small beginning for a much longer and larger process. There are endless possibilities, yet no predetermined directions.

However, no one should assume that there is anything new in a call for such endeavors. The greatest danger for Western, modern and postmodern feminists is to begin by assuming that the question of spirituality is a new direction. In the context of a market-driven model of globalization, there currently exists a seductive ideology of newness in which ideas, actions and various forms of creative processes are valued for their presumed "newness." I have a fearful image of spirituality becoming harnessed as yet another identity to be placed on a list, added to curriculums and titles of anthologies, marketed as a new development in feminist or social thought. This market-driven ideology of newness has little to do with creativity or originality and it has nothing to do with the labor of the disidentified spiritual revolutionary. In fact, new knowledge is never produced; original creations are always a process of placing the mark of one's self on an understanding that is older than time.

What then is the direction of spiritual revolution? I believe that the role of the spiritual revolutionary can never be predetermined or defined to fit a pre-given model. It will always be contingent on one's choices and contextual circumstances and on an element of the unknowable. The spiritual revolutionary is no more than a worker who knows that utopias are real and who, with this knowledge, cannot live but to manifest a world in this image. Such a figure of radical non-violent societal transformation is guided by spiritual principles and by the understanding that such transformation is not simply the ends one aspires to but the very means by which one gains spiritual learning. Mystics are neither omniscient nor infallible. They are human beings unfolding their selves into divinity.

Notes

CHAPTER 1

1. A majority of college students at public institutions are in fact not privileged in the context of the United States but are comparatively privileged from an international perspective. These discrepancies in privilege stem from unequal development and the international division of labor. See Immanuel Wallerstein, *The Capitalist World Economy*, 1979.

2. See Edward Said, *Orientalism*, 1978.

3. For a discussion of this problem from an activist perspective see Farida Shaheed, "The Other Side of Discourse," 1998.

4. See for example Gloria Wekker, "One Finger Does Not Drink Okra Soup," 1997.

5. Throughout this book I address some of the central debates in feminism and feminist writings as they are reflected in contemporary trends in feminist writings and paradigms in the field of Women's Studies. This is not to suggest that feminism is a unitary field of knowledge or activism and throughout the book I draw on feminist scholars, particularly women of color and non-Western feminists, who have in fact challenged such mainstream trends. However, some dominant trends regarding conceptions of theory, practice and the conceptualization of women's rights and interests are discernable both in academic writings as well as in general patterns of student expectations in Women's Studies courses. I refer to these dominant trends as mainstream contemporary feminism in the U.S.

6. This is an important project but not the objective of this book. There is already a rich feminist scholarship which has developed critiques and reinterpretations of various traditions. See for example Judith Plaskow, *Standing Again at Sinai*, 1991; and Amina Wadud, *Quran and Woman*, 1999. For a more controversial approach see work by Mary Daly. In my view, Daly's work rests on an essentialized understanding of women, one that does not examine power relations between women or inequalities of race, nation and class (which also subordinate men).

7. See for example the Dalai Lama, *Ethics for the New Millennium*, 1999; and Andrew Harvey, *Son of Man*, 1999.

8. For a useful response to fears and misconceptions associated with the term "spirituality" see Michael Lerner, *Spirit Matters*, 2000 (particularly Chapter 1).

9. For instance, Chandra Mohanty has argued in her classic essay "Under Western Eyes" (1991) that Western feminist representations were often invested in depicting "Third World" women as victimized objects devoid of agency, thus recolonizing such groups of women by rendering their histories, acts of survival and resistances invisible.

10. There are numerous instances of this process. This was evident for instance in the exclusions of subordinated racial groups and of gays and lesbians from the mainstream labor and women's movements in the United States during the twentieth century.

11. See for instance bell hooks, *Feminist Theory: From Margin to Center*, 1984, for an elaboration of this broad approach to feminism.

12. For a history of the emergence of the notion of secularism, see Owen Chadwick, *The Secularization of the European Mind in the Nineteenth Century*, 1975.

13. Thus while it is often easy for political analysts to point to politicized religious discourse in non-Western contexts, this kind of discourse often goes unmarked in Western contexts like the United States. In the U.S., for instance, it is not limited to organizations such as the Christian Coalition but also permeates the mainstream public sphere. The imagery of good and evil is a vivid example of this moral-religious approach to understanding the world. Such imagery is used by leaders (i.e., the notion of an "axis of evil" put forth by George W. Bush and Ronald Reagan's discourses of the Soviet Union as an "evil empire") but also picked up by the mainstream media. See Laurie Goodstein, "A President Puts His Faith in Providence," *New York Times*, February 9, 2003, p4.

14. A central aspect of my approach rests on an understanding that spirituality is a realm that is as power-laden as the economic, social and cultural realms; hence the strong potential for an abuse of power is always present. I address such issues in chapter 5.

15. Such writers and activists include Jacqui Alexander, Gloria Anzaldúa, Patricia Hill Collins, bell hooks, Audre Lorde and Chandra Mohanty, amongst many others.

16. See Anzaldúa "now let us shift...the path of conocimiento...inner work, public acts," and Jacqui Alexander, "Remembering This Bridge, Remembering Ourselves," in *This Bridge We Call Home*, 2002. See also various other essays in this anthology, in particular AnaLouise Keating, "Charting Pathways, Making Thresholds...A Warning, An Introduction."

17. For example, in Foucault's view, resistance is always defined in relationship to power but it does not transform power. See Foucault, *Power/Knowledge*, 1980. It is as if we have tried to build fences in order to contain and control power just as we have built dams in order to contain and control the flow of water in the earth. The results are similar. Dams produce beautiful green fields for some as they simultaneously devastate other areas by funneling water away from them. Those who own the green fields feel they are victorious, that they have the answer. It is only when such inequities produce a larger crisis—economic and political—that a recognition begins to dawn that this model of control, of separate development, does not work. Such attempts may appear successful in the short run but they merely conceal, distort and eventually pervert the magnificent source from which this power stems. On a related note it is interesting to

note that critics of existing modern forms of economic development have turned to alternative forms of indigenous knowledge and development (see for example Arturo Escobar, *Encountering Development*, 1994) amongst local communities in rural and tribal areas. What is left unexamined is that in such "indigenous" forms the spiritual and material realms are usually not treated as disconnected or oppositional.

18. See Irene Diamond, *Fertile Ground*, 1994, for a critical discussion on feminist usages of the language of control.

19. Once again, even when the dams we build are built for the noblest purposes of progress, they function on an inherent logic of separation that cannot allow for the kinds of transformations which we need so desperately.

20. There are of course numerous critics of the mainly postmodern focus on the links between power and knowledge. My own perspective is one that recognizes the value of postmodern understandings of the nexus between power and knowledge but seeks to go beyond the limiting notion that this relationship cannot be transformed or transcended.

21. Such spiritualized social movements have of course also always existed throughout history. See for instance movements based on liberation theology in Latin America and for discussions of Buddhist liberation movements in Asia see Queen and King, eds., *Engaged Buddhism*, 1996.

CHAPTER 2

1. For instance the inclusion of writings by women, non-Western and non-white scholars and writers has been viewed by conservative (and some liberal) thinkers as a form of "political correctness" which entails a decline in standards. The question of what constitutes a "canon" at institutions of higher education has thus been a question of political debate and conflict.

2. This has not been limited to left resistances. For instance critiques by women of color of the white, Western, middle-class orientation of feminism have also elicited similar resistances from some mainstream feminists. See, for instance, Susan Stanford Friedman's characterization of such intellectual and political critiques by women of color, including writers such as Audre Lorde and Alice Walker, as "scripts of accusation" ("Beyond White and Other," 1995). The reduction of these challenges to the language of accusation rests on the assumption that white women must personally identify with racial privilege, thereby feeling "accused" by women of color.

3. See Evelyn Nakano Glenn, *Unequal Freedom*, 2002.

4. See for example Nancy Fraser, *Justice Interruptus*, 1996. She attempts to separate out questions of recognition (linked to identity) and questions of redistribution (presumably linked to socioeconomic inequality).

5. For instance, in the current moment, the mobilization of Muslim and Arab Americans is of fundamental importance in light of the intense racial targeting of this group. The point is not that such identity-based mobilizations are not

often necessary and critical political forces for equality. However, my intention is to deal with a broader question of social transformation.

6. There is a vast scholarship that demonstrates this. See for example bell hooks, *Feminist Theory: From Margin to Center*, 1984; Jacqui Alexander, "Not Just Any(Body) Can be a Citizen," 1994; Patricia Williams, *The Alchemy of Race and Rights*, 1991.

7. This is not to suggest that hegemonic national identity is the same as the identity-based activism of subordinated sexual, racial and ethnic groups, as the latter are acting in an attempt to transform relationships of power while the former represents a hegemonic identity. My point is simply to underscore the underlying logic of identification at work.

8. See "The Theoretical Subject of *This Bridge Called My Back* and Anglo American Feminism," 1990.

9. For a discussion of how this affects classroom dynamics see Cervanek, Cespedes, Souza and Straub, "Imagining Differently," 2002.

10. See for example Judith Butler, *Gender Trouble*, 1990; Kimberle Crenshaw, "Mapping the Margins," 1994; Trinh T. Minh-ha, *Woman, Native, Other*, 1989; Patricia Hill Collins, *Black Feminist Thought*, 1990; amongst many others.

11. See Alarcón, 1990, for a discussion of this as well as how the feminist attachment to gender identity reproduces this misrepresentation.

12. AnaLouise Keating, "Charting Pathways" in Anzaldúa and Keating, eds., *This Bridge We Call Home*, 2002, 11.

13. Lorde, *Sister Outsider*, 1984, 110.

14. For a theoretical discussion of the concept of disidentification see Rosemary Hennessy, *Materialist Feminism and the Politics of Discourse*, 1992, especially p. 96.

15. See also AnaLouise Keating, "Forging El Mundo Zurdo," 2002, 529, for a discussion of the vulnerability that results from letting go of labels.

16. This point is in reference to mainstream contemporary feminist writing, activism and discourse. There has of course always been a stream within feminism which has addressed spirituality. For an overview see Judith Plaskow and Carol Christ, eds., *Weaving the Visions: New Patterns in Feminist Spirituality*, 1989.

17. There is always a tendency for academics to dismiss popular culture without understanding the kind of need something like *Oprah* is responding to. For a specific discussion of *Oprah*, race and spirituality see Hull, *Soul Talk*, 2001.

18. See Diana Fuss, *Essentially Speaking*, 1989.

19. See *Woman, Native, Other*, 1989, 94.

20. Alexander, "Remembering *This Bridge*, Remembering Ourselves," 2002, 99.

21. Too often scholars and activists have used a return to claims of universalism

as a means to dismiss or evade the ways in which issues such as race and colonialism complicate and shape social relationships. See for example Susan Okin, "Feminism, Women's Human Rights and Cultural Differences," 2000.

22. I first came to this example by reading Drucilla Cornell's interpretation of Wekker's essay in *At the Heart of Freedom,* 1998; my interpretation takes a different direction.

23. See Alarcón, 1990, for a critique of such usages.

24. For a discussion of spirituality in Anzaldúa's work and especially Anzaldúa's own views on how this dimension has been neglected by readers see Gloria Anzaldúa, *Interviews,* 2000.

25. For instance, in India, goddess worship in Hinduism has been incorporated into patriarchal conceptions of Hindu nationalism, while Western feminist celebrations of goddess worship often extract such indigenous spiritual traditions from their historical, political and economic contexts and reduce them to more essentialized forms of "feminine" power.

26. See *Gender Trouble,* 143.

27. For an overview of such debates see Linda Nicholson, ed., *Feminism/Postmodernism,* 1990.

CHAPTER 3

1. I use the term "Third World" here to include Latin America, Asia and Africa. The use of the term, in my understanding, embodies shared histories of colonialism and unequal relationships of power within the current world order.

2. For early works that raised these challenges see Cherríe Moraga and Gloria Anzaldúa, eds., *This Bridge Called My Back,* 1981; bell hooks, *Feminist Theory: From Margin to Center,* 1984; Gloria T. Hull, Patricia Bell Scott and Barbara Smith, eds., *All the women are White, all the Blacks are men, but some of us are brave,* 1982.

3. Such criticisms have been made in both theoretical and activist debates. See for instance Chandra Mohanty's critique of the ways in which the language of a presumed global sisterhood used by feminists such as Robin Morgan have overlooked and often reproduced hierarchies of race and nation that shape women's lives and underlie relationships between groups of women from different social contexts ("Feminist Encounters," 1992). For a more recent discussion of the persistence of such problems see Uma Narayan, *Dislocating Cultures,* 1997; and Tani Barlow, "International Feminism of the Future," 2000. For a discussion of the effects of such relationships of power for transnational feminist activism see Sonia Alvarez, "Translating the Global: Effects of Transnational Organizing on Local Feminist Discourses and Practices in Latin America," 2000; and Amrita Basu, "Globalization of the Local/Localization of the Global: Mapping Transnational Women's Movements," 2000.

4. See Rita Raj, ed., *Women at the Intersection,* 2002. For a discussion of this concept of "intersectionality" see Kimberle Crenshaw, "Mapping the Margins," 1994.

5. For instance, both print and television media representations were rife with images of veiled Afghani women during the military campaign and of women unveiling themselves (mainly in Kabul) after the defeat of the Taliban. While feminist organizations had mobilized to publicize the severe repression of women under the Taliban long before September 11, these mobilizations and issues had never gained extensive media attention prior to the U.S. military campaign in Afghanistan. This contradiction has been further underlined by the fact that women's interests and representation have been marginalized in the formation of the new government in Afghanistan. Unlike the media focus on veiling, this marginalization has received little mainstream media attention. Note that Afghanistan's well-known women's organization, RAWA (Revolutionary Association of the Women of Afghanistan), condemned the military campaign. See for example "Let Us Struggle Against War and Fundamentalism and For Peace and Democracy," RAWA's statement on International Women's Day, March 8, 2002, http://rawa.false.net/mar8-02en.htm.

6. See Leila Ahmed, *Gender and Islam,* 1992; Lata Mani, "Contentious Traditions," 1998; and Chandra Mohanty, "Under Western Eyes," 1991.

7. Jeffrey and Basu, *Appropriating Gender,* 1998; McClintock, *Imperial Leather,* 1995.

8. For instance, issues such as female genital mutilation, veiling and dowry deaths operate as symbols of oppressive non-Western cultures. See Narayan, *Dislocating Cultures,* 1997, for a discussion of this as well as Chandra Mohanty's earlier text, "Under Western Eyes," 1991. The power of such representations has unfortunately not dissipated despite such critical perspectives written by feminists both internationally and in the U.S.

9. This is not to say that there are no instances of positive alliances or shared interests between U.S. and non-Western women. Nor is it to say that U.S. agendas are not challenged; there have often been intellectual and political challenges to U.S. agendas posed by non-Western feminists in international contexts. However, instances of having to mount such challenges also points to the dominance of U.S. agendas. Such questions of power and control also permeate feminist practice within different countries as privileges of class, education, language, ethnicity, caste and religion may shape organizational structures and agendas.

10. For a classic text on this issue see Elizabeth Spelman, *Inessential Woman,* 1988.

11. For an important discussion on the ways in which resistance to theory can obstruct deeper discussions of race and identity in the classroom see Sara Cervenak, Karina Cespedes, Caridad Souza and Andrea Staub, "Imagining Differently: The Politics of Listening in a Feminist Classroom," 2002.

12. One student put it to me quite bluntly in the discussion of an historical analysis of paid reproductive work by women of color in the U.S. when she asked why we had to spend so much time on issues of race when these were such "old issues."

13. I am referring here to the material violence of poverty. For a discussion of poverty as a form of structural violence see Paul Farmer, "On Suffering and Structural Violence," 1997.

14. The Dalai Lama might seem like an unusual starting point for a discussion of feminist practice but in fact this starting point is not far from the approaches of many feminist thinkers who have used ethical appeals in defense of women's rights. Consider for instance Drucilla Cornell's vision of the idea of an imaginary domain as a sovereign space necessary for the preservation of women's (and men's) sexual and personal freedom. In *At the Heart of Freedom*, 1998, Cornell writes of her need to "defend the sanctuary of the imaginary domain by an ethical appeal to our need for the moral and psychic space in which to orient ourselves sexually. By ethical, I mean the practice of trying to figure out our vision of the good life. The claim for the imaginary domain is that it gives each of us the chance to become a unique person"(28). In this line of reasoning, Cornell is using a notion of ethical practice as a means for undergirding the right to sexual and social freedom, particularly in relation to patriarchal, heterosexual ideologies and legal strictures that seek to restrict such freedom.

15. Foucault, *The History of Sexuality,* 1978.

16. *The Tibetan Book of Living and Dying,* 1994, 209.

17. *Soul Talk,* 2001, 81.

18. See Collins, "Searching for Sojourner Truth," 1998.

19. "Uses of the Erotic: The Erotic As Power," 1989, 210.

20. See *Sister Outsider,* 1984. For a breaking of such boundaries see for example "Uses of the Erotic: The Erotic As Power."

21. AnaLouise Keating, "Charting Pathways, Making Thresholds," 2002, 8.

22. See bell hooks, *All About Love,* 2000, for an important discussion of the misconceptions of the meaning of "love" in contemporary U.S. society.

23. *Non-Violent Resistance,* 2001, 75.

24. In fact, he argued in his writings that if people were not ready for this transformative sense of non-violence, it would be preferable to use force in self-defense.

25. Ibid., p38.

26. See Amita Baviskar "Written on the Body, Written on the Land: Violence and Environmental Struggles in Central India," 2001. Strategies of non-violence that have drawn on spiritualized understandings of the world have often shaped indigenous movements for environmental and social justice. Other examples include the Chipko movement in India that aimed to prevent deforestation,

Native American movements in the United States, and indigenous movements in Latin America.

27. For a vivid depiction of this movement see the documentary film *A Narmada Diary* by Anand Patwardhan and Simantini Dhuru, 1995.

28. See Gila Svirsky, Women in Black and Coalition of Women for Peace, "Address to the Security Council," October 23, 2002, http://shalomctr.org/html/peace125.html.

29. See "Text and Action from Rabbis for Human Rights," http://www.shalomctr.org/html/peace28.html.

30. Note there have been many important criticisms of Gandhi. Such criticisms include his conservative approach to questions of sexuality, his paternalistic approach to his social upliftment programs with the low caste "untouchables" (named by Gandhi as Harijans but now self-named as dalits) and, most significantly, his use of Hindu religious symbols and language in ways which alienated Muslims. While Gandhi ultimately believed in and struggled for religious harmony, his use of Hindu religious traditions often overlooked the ways in which they recoded relationships of power between Hindus and Muslims. While scholarly discussions and criticisms of Gandhi are vast, his deeper insights of the transformative possibilities of spirituality and social justice have often been lost in academic analyses.

31. Gandhi's understanding of independence was starkly different from those of other nationalist leaders of his time; independence was not a narrowly political objective in his understanding. See his writings in *Hind Swaraj*, 1997 edition.

32. Critics of Gandhi have often read this as a form of political conservatism. There are important criticisms to be made with regard to the ways in which Gandhi failed to adequately challenge class inequalities, particularly in the ways in which he attempted to reconcile the interests of peasants and workers with the middle classes and bourgeoisie in India. However, to reduce Gandhi's philosophy of non-violence to an assumption of class-based reformism is to miss a deeper consideration of his understanding of social transformation. For resources on Gandhi's work in the U.S. see the M.K. Gandhi Institute for Non-violence, www.gandhiinstitute.org.

33. See for example Margaret Bacon, *Mothers of Feminism: The Story of Quaker Women in America*, 1986, and *The Quiet Rebels*, 2000; and Elisabeth Potts Brown and Susan Stuard, eds., *Witnesses for Change: Quaker Women Over Three Centuries*, 1989.

34. Quaker women were imprisoned and beaten for speaking out about spiritual and social equality for women. Margaret Bacon describes such repression at length, including cases where, for example, Quaker women travelling to New England were viewed as being so threatening they were stripped naked and imprisoned. See *Mothers of Feminism*, 25.

35. Note that Marx's theories did go beyond a purely economic analysis. See for example his discussion of the concept of alienation.

36. See for instance Gramsci's brief discussion of such an alternative state in the section "Statolatory" of his writings in the *Prison Notebooks*, 1971. He speaks of the need to form an alternative form of state, yet does not provide specific discussions of its form or underlying principles that would render this state different from existing forms of state power. It is perhaps not surprising that actual leftist alternatives have rested more on policy changes (for instance regarding state intervention in redistribution) and on changing the social basis of the state (that is, which groups or classes hold power) than on developing a real alternative kind of state.

37. This is of course not a new process. Consider for instance the prevalence of racial profiling and high levels of policing of African Americans. What has changed now is the scale, as this foresaking of the principles and protections of democratic freedom is now in the name of "national security."

38. Such dynamics also characterized state responses to the military campaign against Afghanistan. The fact that there are still no official estimates of Afghan civilian casualties is itself a telling reflection of the ways in which life is valued and undervalued through processes of racial and national ideologies. For an estimate of casualties and an analysis of such processes see Marc Herrold, "A Dossier on Civilian Victims of United States' Aeriel Bombing of Afghanistan: A Comprehensive Accounting," 2001.

39. See http://peacefultomorrows.org for more on this organization.

40. King, *A Testament of Hope*, 1986, 19.

41. Ibid., 47.

42. See Dennis, Golden and Wright, *Oscar Romero*, 2001, 52.

43. Ibid., 71.

44. Ibid., 73-74.

45. See Renny Golden, *The Hour of the Poor, the Hour of Women*, 1991.

46. Ibid., 35.

47. See for example W.E.B. du Bois, *The Souls of Black Folk*, 1997; bell hooks, *Feminist Theory: From Margin to Center*, 1984; Joan Kelly, *Women, History and Theory*, 1984.

48. See essays in the collection, Anzaldúa, ed., *Making Face, Making Soul*, 1990.

49. It was not a coincidence that Gandhi wanted the Indian Nationalist Congress organization to disband after India achieved independence from the British in 1947. Skeptics then and now would of course dismiss this disbanding as impractical or unrealistic. Yet one might wonder how contemporary India might look if it had not had to deal with the hegemony of a single political party (the Congress party) for most of the first few decades of independence. There are many examples of this kind. For instance: socialist organizations whose character completely changed in countries where they gained power and became affiliated with state structures; trade unions which have become overly

institutionalized as bargaining agents and have lost grassroots connections with workers; women's organizations and non-governmental organizations which are "donor-driven," that is, which organize programs and agendas in order to fit the frameworks of and receive funds from international aid organizations rather than build on the grassroots agendas of their targeted constituencies. I have also experienced this in the academy, where there is a corporate-style pressure to create visible feminist programs in order to apply for money from various sources rather than the reverse process of first thinking about what kinds of activities are meaningful and needed, and then searching for resources to carry them out.

CHAPTER 4

1. Such links between power and knowledge cover a broad range of issues including media representations of non-Western cultures and politics, the ways in which cultural representations such as film and television shows encode power relationships (see Trinh T. Minh-ha, *When the Moon Waxes Red,* 1991; Fatimah Rony, *The Third Eye,* 1996), and the ways in which, historically, knowledge about non-Western nations has been inextricably linked with processes of colonialism (Said, *Orientalism,* 1978).

2. See for example Lata Mani's discussion of sati (widow immolation) in *Contentious Traditions,* 1998; and Veena Oldenberg's discussion of female infanticide and dowry in India in *Dowry Murder,* 2002.

3. Spivak, "Can the Subaltern Speak?" 1988; Trinh T. Minh-ha, *Woman, Native, Other,* 1989, and *When the Moon Waxes Red,* 1991.

4. Ruth Behar, *Translated Woman,* 1993; Diane Wolf, ed., *Feminist Dilemmas in Fieldwork,* 1994; Kamala Visweswaran, "Betrayal," 1994.

5. This panic is often most acute amongst students who are themselves originally from the communities or countries they are going to study.

6. See for instance Nicholas Dirks, "Colonial Histories and Native Informants: A Biography of an Archive,"1993, on the political processes involved in the construction of the archive in colonial India. Note that these dynamics are not limited to the social sciences and humanities. For a discussion of the sciences see Karen Barad, "Meeting the Universe Halfway," 1996.

7. An example would be the role of the U.S. in promoting free market economic policies that have had harsh effects on less-privileged women.

8. The argument usually rests on the assumption that the focus on knowledge production is overly academic or theoretical and not relevant to the lives of real women outside of the academy. There are of course problems when Women's Studies exclusively focuses on knowledge production, but the dynamics in fields such as Women's Studies usually produce polarized camps—i.e., those who focus on theory/knowledge production and those who focus on practice. I am contesting the very foundations of this dichotomy.

9. This also fundamentally differs from notions of empathy which are sometimes deployed by ethnographers. The notion of empathy can sometimes be

used in ways that overlook the power-laden dimensions of this relationship and responsibility.

10. See for example Rosetta Ross, *Witnessing and Testifying*, 2003; *Felman and Laub, Testimony*, 1992; John Beverly, *Against Literature*, 1993.

11. In Felman and Laub, *Testimony*, 1992, 110.

12. Ibid.

13. In some cases, certain strategies could help change material aspects of the lives in question—for instance through participatory research which directly engages concerns of the group or community in question; the point is not to ignore such kinds of possibilities.

14. It should not of course end here if knowledge is to be linked to broader social transformation.

15. Ruth Behar, *Translated Woman*, 1993.

16. *Betrayal*, 1994.

17. My understanding of some of these questions was deepened by papers presented and discussed at the conference "Sociological Perspectives on the Holocaust and Post-Holocaust Jewish Life," New Brunswick, 2001.

18. Over a decade of teaching in Women's Studies has shown me that such approaches can be particularly problematic when taken to an extreme because they can enable a sense of arrogance amongst students which has nothing to do with participatory learning and teaching. In such cases, I have found that students often mistake opinion for learning. They are in effect entrenched in a liberal ideology which confuses the importance of each student developing her own critical perspective with the assumption that all opinions are of equal merit. Such problems are compounded by a market-driven approach to education where students are explicitly constructed by universities as consumers of knowledge. The effects of such an approach trickle down into the classroom in ways that induce students to expect that education will be entertaining, when actually, learning about oppression and inequality is a painstaking process that may substantially shake students' worldviews, a process that is far from comforting.

19. See Shiva, 2001. Acts of theft also abound in the daily actions of individuals. There is unfortunately a prevalence of conscious acts of plagiarism amongst intellectuals, including those who produce discourses regarding questions of power, feminism, colonialism and other social issues.

20. There is now a vast literature in post-colonial studies which addresses such issues. See for example Dipesh Chakrabarty, *Provincializing Europe*, 2000.

21. The term "traditional intellectuals" is used by Gramsci, *Prison Notebooks*, 1971, to refer to intellectuals within academic institutions.

22. See for example Donna Haraway, "Situated Knowledges," 1988.

1. Such critics speak from a variety of philosophical and ideological positions and should not be generalized as religious nationalists. See for example Dharma Kumar, "Left Secularists and Communalism," 1994; Partha Chatterjee, "Secularism and Toleration," 1994; T.N. Madan, "Secularism in Its Place," 1987; Ashis Nandy, "The Politics of Secularism and the Recovery of Religious Tolerance," 1990.

2. For criticisms and alternative readings see for instance Judith Plaskow, *Standing Again At Sinai*, 1991; Andrew Harvey, *Son of Man*, 1999; Michael Lerner, *Jewish Renewal*, 1994. See also various writings on Sufi mysticism. For useful overviews and introductions see Idries Shah, *The Sufis*, 1971; and Margaret Smith, *Readings from the Mystics of Islam*, 1994.

3. Such as the rise of Hindu nationalism in India, Jewish religious fundamentalism in Israel and amongst settler communities in the occupied West Bank and Gaza, and Christian fundamentalism in the United States.

4. Note that conceptions of secularism vary. In the United States, for instance, it rests on a notion of a clear separation between church and state; in India secularism has rested more on a notion of preserving the equal rights of different religious communities—for example, minority communities such as Muslims are allowed to follow their own community laws in family and personal matters such as marriage, divorce and inheritance. It is also important to note that even officially secular countries in the West usually implicitly encode religious-based traditions and beliefs in the public sphere of both state and civil society.

5. See for instance the preoccupation of Western feminists with questions such as veiling in Islam, the harem in the Middle East and sati in India.

6. It is this fact that the secular left has historically tended to underestimate and overlook in terms of its own confrontation, or lack thereof, with matters of the spirit.

7. The contemporary Hindu nationalist movement (referred to as the Hindutva movement) has produced a territorialized definition of religion in India. According to Hindutva ideology, the only authentic Indian religions are those that arose within the geographical boundaries of India (for example Hinduism, Sikhism, Jainism). Christianity and Islam are termed "foreign" because they did not originate within the Indian subcontinent.

8. See for instance the Bhagavad Gita on this conception of the Self.

9. For important works see Thomas Hansen, *The Saffron Wave*, 1999; Patricia Jeffrey and Amrita Basu, eds., *Appropriating Gender*, 1998; Tanika Sarkar, *Hindu Wife, Hindu Nation*, 2002.

10. *Son of Man*, 1999, 76.

11. For a discussion of the privatization of spirituality in the United States see Michael Lerner, *Spirit Matters*, 2000.

12. This is not to imply that such spaces do not serve as important sources of

support and guidance for many individuals. However, I want to point to the larger political and structural implications.

13. Sheela Raval, "Lifestyle: New Age Healing," *India Today,* January 21, 2002: 38-41. The commercialized organization of the healing industry has emerged as part of broader processes of globalization and it is distinctive from longstanding indigenous practices of healing and local knowledges that have always existed in India.

14. Such dismissals can also be used to mischaracterize spiritual teachings of those who challenge the power bases of existing religious institutions.

15. There is also a trend in the United States of extreme anti-Islam sentiments and increasing censorship preventing the kind of reclaiming of Islam that is needed. See for instance the outcry that occurred soon after 9/11 against the Harvard student attempting to reclaim the term "jihad" and restore it to its original meaning of "internal struggle."

16. From a spiritual perspective, security can never ultimately reside in the bounded form of a nation-state.

17. See, for example, the organization of families of 9/11 victims in "Peaceful Tomorrows," which I describe in chapter 3.

18. I am of course including individuals within the U.S. as those who may express such frustration. My discussion of "American" throughout this book refers to a hegemonic nationalist perspective that may not include the views of many who live in the U.S.

19. Consider for example the ways in which the mainstream media and many political leaders used the need to protect Americans to dismiss the massive protests against the war on Iraq.

20. This unravelling is inherent in the growing loss of civil society in the wake of the attacks as the mainstream public has willingly embraced encroachments on civil liberties. The notion of needing to build civil society has been a central theme in political science scholarship on democratization in Eastern Europe, Asia, Africa and Latin America. It is ironic that with such attention to building democracy in other contexts, the reversal of democratization and the gradual dismantling of civil society has received comparatively little mainstream public concern. There has however been serious work done by non-governmental organizations such as the ACLU and immigrant organizations representing Arab Americans and other targeted groups.

21. I use "mainstream" here to contrast conservative church structures to alternative practices, such as those that adhere to some form of liberation theology.

22. *Saffron Wave,* 1999, 162.

23. For a discussion of the need for spiritual regeneration see also bell hooks, *Salvation,* 2001.

Abu-Lughod, Lila. 1990. "The Romance of Resistance: Tracing Transformations of Power Through Bedouin Women." *American Ethnologist* 17, no. 3: 41-55.

Ahmed, Leila. 1992. *Women and Gender in Islam: Historical Roots of a Modern Debate.* New Haven: Yale University Press.

Alarcón, Norma. 1990. "The Theoretical Subjects of This Bridge Called My Back and Anglo American Feminism." In Gloria Anzaldúa, ed., *Making Face, Making Soul: Haciendo Caras.* San Francisco: Aunt Lute Books. 356-69.

Alexander, Jacqui. 1994. "Not Just (Any)Body Can Be a Citizen: The Politics of Law, Sexuality and Postcoloniality in Trinidad and Tobago and the Bahamas." *Feminist Review* 48:5-23.

_____. 2002. "Remembering *This Bridge*, Remembering Ourselves." In Gloria Anzaldúa and AnaLouise Keating, eds., *This Bridge We Call Home.* New York: Routledge. 81-103.

Alvarez, Sonia. 2000. "Translating the Global: Effects of Transnational Organizing of Local Feminist Discourses and Practices in Latin America." *Meridians* 1, no. 1: 29-67.

Anzaldúa, Gloria. 1987. *Borderlands/La Frontera: The New Mestiza.* San Francisco: Aunt Lute Books.

_____. 2002. *Interviews.* New York: Routledge.

_____., ed. 1990. *Making Face, Making Soul: Haciendo Caras.* San Francisco: Aunt Lute Books.

_____. 2002. "now let us shift...the path of conocimiento...inner work, public acts." In Gloria Anzaldúa and AnaLouise Keating, eds., *This Bridge We Call Home.* New York: Routledge. 540-578.

_____. and AnaLouise Keating, eds. 2002. *This Bridge We Call Home.* New York: Routledge.

Bacon, Margaret Hope. 1986. *The Mothers of Feminism: The Story of Quaker Women in America.* New York: Harper Collins.

_____. 2000. *The Quiet Rebels: The Story of Quakers in America.* Wallingford, PA: Pendle Hill Publications.

Barad, Karen. 1996. "Meeting the Universe Halfway: Realism and Social Constructivism Without Contradiction." In Lynn Hankinson. Nelson and

Jack Nelson, eds., *Feminism, Science and the Philosophy of Science.* Dordrecht, Holland: Kluwer Press. 161-193.

Barlow, Tani. 2000. "International Feminism of the Future." *Signs: A Journal of Women, Culture and Society* 25, no. 4: 1099-1105.

Basu, Amrita. 2000. "Globalization of the Local/Localization of the Global: Mapping Transnational Women's Movements." *Meridians* 1, no. 1 :68-84.

Baviskar, Amita. 2001. "Written on the Body, Written on the Land: Violence and Environmental Struggles in Central India." In Nancy Lee Peluso and Michael Watts, eds., *Violent Environments.* Ithaca: Cornell University Press. 354-379.

Behar, Ruth. 1993. *Translated Woman: Crossing the Border With Esperanza's Story.* Boston: Beacon Press.

Berlant, Lauren. 1997. *The Queen of America Goes to Washington City: Essays on Sex and Citizenship.* Durham, NC: Duke University Press.

Bharucha, Rustom. 1993. *The Question of Faith.* New Delhi: Orient Longman.

Brown, Elizabeth Potts and Susan Stuard, eds. 1989. *Witness for Change: Quaker Women Over Three Centuries.* Piscataway, NJ: Rutgers University Press.

Butler, Judith. 1990. *Gender Trouble.* New York: Routledge.

Cervenak, Sara, Karina Cespedes, Caridad Souza and Andrea Staub. 2002. "Imagining Differently: The Politics of Listening in a Feminist Classroom." In Gloria Anzaldúa and AnaLouise Keating, eds., *This Bridge We Call Home.* New York: Routledge. 341-356.

Chadwick, Owen. 1975. *The Secularization of the European Mind in the Nineteenth Century.* Cambridge: Cambridge University Press.

Chakrabarty, Dipesh. 2000. *Provincializing Europe.* Princeton, NJ: Princeton University Press.

Chatterjee, Partha. 1994. "Secularism and Toleration," *Economic and Political Weekly* July 9: 1768-1777.

Collins, Patricia Hill. 1990. *Black Feminist Thought.* New York: Routledge.

———. 1998. "Searching for Sojourner Truth." In Collins, ed., *Fighting Words: Black Women and the Search for Justice.* Minneapolis: University of Minnesota Press. 229-251.

Cornell, Drucilla. 1998. *At the Heart of Freedom: Feminism, Sex and Equality.* Princeton, NJ: Princeton University Press.

Crenshaw, Kimberle. 1994. "Mapping the Margins: Intersectionality, Identity Politics and Violence Against Women of Color." In Roxanne Myktiuk, Martha Albertson and Martha Fineman eds., *In the Public Nature of Private Violence: The Discovery of Domestic Abuse*. New York: Routledge. 93-118.

Dalai Lama. 1999. *Ethics for the New Millenium*. New York: Riverhead Books.

Dennis, Marie, Renny Golden and Scott Wright. 2000. *Oscar Romero*. New York: Orbis Books.

Diamond, Irene. 1994. *Fertile Ground: Women, Earth and the Limits of Control*. Boston: Beacon Press.

Dirks, Nicholas. 1993. "Colonial Histories and Native Informants: A Biography of an Archive." In Carol Breckenridge and Peter van der Veer, eds., *Orientalism and the Postcolonial Predicament*. Philadelphia: University of Pennsylvania Press. 279-313.

du Bois, W.E.B. 1997 ed. *The Souls of Black Folk*. Boston: Bedford Books.

Enloe, Cynthia. 2000. *Maneuvers: The International Politics of Militarizing Women's Lives*. Berkeley: University of California Press.

Farmer, Paul. 1997. "On Suffering and Structural Violence." In Arthur Kleinman, Veena Das and Margaret Lock, eds., *Social Suffering*. Berkeley: University of California Press. 261-283.

Felman, Shoshana and Dori Laub. 1992. *Testimony: Crises of Witnessing in Literature, Psychoanalysis, and History*. New York: Routledge.

Foucault, Michel. 1978. *The History of Sexuality: An Introduction*. Vol. 1. Trans. Robert Hurley. New York: Vintage Books.

_____. 1980. *Power/Knowledge: Selected Interviews and Other Writings, 1972-1977*. Trans. Alan Sheridan. New York: Pantheon Books.

Fraser, Nancy. 1996. *Justice Interruptus: Critical Reflections on the "Postsocialist" Condition*. New York: Routledge.

Friedman, Susan Stanford. 1995. "Beyond White and Other: Relationality and Narratives of Race in Feminist Discourse." *Signs: A Journal of Women, Culture and Society* 21 (Autumn): 1-49.

Fuss, Diana. 1990. *Essentially Speaking: Feminism, Nature and Difference*. New York: Routledge and Kegan Paul.

Gandhi, Mohandas. 2001 ed. *Non-Violent Resistance (Satyagraha)*. New York: Dover Publications.

_____. 1997. *Hind Swaraj and Other Writings*. Edited by Anthony Parel. Cambridge: Cambridge University Press.

Glenn, Evelyn Nakano. 2002. *Unequal Freedom*. Cambridge, MA: Harvard University Press.

Golden, Renny. 1991. *The Hour of the Poor, the Hour of Women: Salvadoran Women Speak*. New York: Crossroad/Herder & Herder.

Gramsci, Antonio. 1971. *Selections from the Prison Notebooks*. Trans. Quinton Hoare and G.N. Smith. New York: International Publishers.

Griffiths, Bede. 1976. *Return to the Center*. Springfield, IL: Templegate.

Hancock, E. Lee. 1999. *The Book of Women's Sermons: Hearing God in Each Other's Voices*. New York: Riverhead.

Hanson, Thomas. 1999. *The Saffron Wave: Democracy and Hindu Nationalism in India*. Princeton, NJ: Princeton University Press.

Haraway, Donna. 1988. "Situated Knowledges: The Science Question in Feminism and the Privilege of Partial Perspective." *Feminist Studies* 14 (Fall): 575-596.

Harvey, Andrew. 1999. *Son of Man: The Mystical Path to Christ*. New York: Putnam.

Hennessy, Rosemary. 1992. *Materialist Feminism and the Politics of Discourse*. New York: Routledge.

Herrold, Marc, 2001. "A Dossier on Civilian Victims of United States' Aerial Bombing of Afghanistan: A Comprehensive Accounting." http://cursor.org/stories/civilian_deaths.htm.

_____. 2002. "U.S. Bombing and Afghan Civilian Deaths: The Official Neglect of 'Unworthy' Bodies." *International Journal of Urban and Regional Research* 26 (3): 626-634.

hooks, bell. 1984. *Feminist Theory: From Margin to Center*. Boston: South End Press.

_____. 2000. *All About Love: New Visions*. New York: Harper Collins.

_____. 2001. *Salvation: Black People and Love*. New York: Harper Collins.

Hull, Gloria T. 2001. *Soul Talk: The New Spirituality of African American Women*. Vermont: Inner Traditions.

_____., Patricia Bell Scott and Barbara Smith, eds. 1982. *All the women are White, all the Blacks are men, but some of us are brave: Black women's studies*. Old Westbury, NY: Feminist Press, 1982.

Jeffrey, Patricia and Amrita Basu. 1998. *Appropriating Gender: Women's Activism and Politicized Religion in South Asia*. New York: Routledge.

Keating, AnaLouise. 2002. "Forging El Mundo Zurdo: Changing Ourselves, Changing the World." In Gloria Anzaldúa and AnaLouise Keating, eds., *This Bridge We Call Home*. New York: Routledge. 519-530.

_____. 2002. "Charting Pathways, Making Thresholds...A Warning, An Introduction." In Gloria Anzaldúa and AnaLouise Keating, eds., *This Bridge We Call Home*. New York: Routledge. 6-20.

Kelly, Joan. 1984. *Women, History and Theory*. Chicago: University of Chicago Press.

King, Martin Luther, Jr. 1986. *A Testament of Hope: The Essential Writings and Speeches of Martin Luther King, Jr*. Edited by James Washington. San Francisco: Harper Collins.

Kumar, Dharma. 1994. "Left Secularists and Communalists." *Economic and Political Weekly* July 9: 1803-1809.

Lerner, Michael. 1994. *Jewish Renewal: A Path to Healing and Transformation*. New York: Putnam.

_____. 2000. *Spirit Matters*. Charlottesville, VA: Hampton Roads.

Lorde, Audre. 1985. *Sister Outsider: Essays and Speeches*. New York: Kitchen Table/Women of Color Press.

_____. 1989. "Uses of the Erotic: The Erotic As Power." In Judith Plaskow and Carol P. Christ, eds., *Weaving the Visions: New Patterns in Feminist Spirituality*. San Francisco: Harper Collins. 208-213.

Madan, T.N. 1987. "Secularism in its Place." *Journal of Asian Studies* 46, no. 4: 747-759.

Mani, Lata. 1989. "Contentious Traditions: The Debate on Sati in Colonial India." In Kumkum Sangari and Sudesh Vaid, eds., *Recasting Women: Essays in Colonial History*. New Brunswick: Rutgers University Press. 88-126.

_____. 1998. *Contentious Traditions: The Debate on Sati in Colonial India*. Berkeley: University of California Press.

Marx, Karl. 1995 edition. *Capital: An Abridged Edition*. Edited by David McClellan. Oxford: Oxford University Press.

McClintock, Anne. 1995. *Imperial Leather: Race, Gender and Sexuality in the Colonial Context.* New York: Routledge.

Mies, Maria. 1986. *Patriarchy and Accumulation on a World Scale.* Atlantic Highlands, NJ: Zed Books.

Mohanty, Chandra. 1991. "Under Western Eyes." In Chandra Mohanty, Ann Russo and Lourdes Torres, eds., *Third World Women and the Politics of Feminism.* Bloomington: Indiana University Press. 51-80.

———. 1992. "Feminist Encounters: Locating the Politics of Experience." In Michele Barrett and Anne Phillips, eds., *Destabilizing Theory: Contemporary Feminist Debates.* Stanford, CA: Stanford University Press. 74-92.

Moraga, Cherríe and Gloria Anzaldúa, eds. 1983. 2nd edition. *This Bridge Called My Back: Writings by Radical Women of Color.* New York: Kitchen Table/Women of Color Press.

Nandy, Ashis, 1990. "The Politics of Secularism and the Recovery of Religious Tolerance." In Veena Das, ed., *Mirrors of Violence.* New Delhi: Oxford University Press. 69-93.

Narayan, Uma. 1997. *Dislocating Cultures: Identities, Traditions and Third World Feminism.* New York: Routledge.

Nicholson, Linda J., ed. 1990. *Feminism/Postmodernism.* New York: Routledge.

Okin, Susan. 2000. "Feminism, Women's Human Rights and Cultural Differences." In Narayan and Harding, eds., *Decentering the Center: Philosophy for a Multicultural, Postcolonial and Feminist World.* Bloomington: Indiana University Press. 26-46.

Oldenberg, Veena Talwar. 2002. *Dowry Murder: The Imperial Origins of a Cultural Crime.* New York: Oxford University Press.

Plaskow, Judith. 1991. *Standing Again At Sinai: Judaism from a Feminist Perspective.* New York: Harper Collins.

———. and Carol Christ, eds. 1989. *Weaving the Visions: New Patterns in Feminist Spirituality.* New York: Harper Collins.

Queen, Christopher and Sallie King, eds. 1996. *Engaged Buddhism: Buddhist Liberation Movements in Asia.* Albany: State University of New York Press.

Rinpoche, Sogyal. 1994. *The Tibetan Book of Living and Dying.* San Francisco: Harper Collins.

Rony, Fatimah. 1996. *The Third Eye: Race, Cinema and Ethnographic Spectacle.* Durham, NC: Duke University Press.

Ross, Rosetta. *Witnessing and Testifying: Black Women, Religion and Civil Rights.* Minneapolis: Fortress Press.

Sacks, Karen. 1990. "Towards a Unified Theory of Race, Class and Gender." *American Ethnologist* 17: 534-550.

Said, Edward. 1978. *Orientalism.* New York: Pantheon Books.

Sarkar, Tanika. 2002. *Hindu Wife, Hindu Nation: Community, Religion and Cultural Nationalism.* Bloomington: Indiana University Press.

Sarkar, Tanika and Urvashi Butalia. 1995. *Women and the Hindu Right: A Collection of Essays.* New Delhi: Kali for Women.

Shah, Idries. 1971. *The Sufis.* New York: Random House.

Shiva, Vandana. 2001. *Protect or Plunder? Understanding Intellectual Property Rights.* New York: Zed Books.

Smith, Margaret. 1994. *Readings from the Mystics of Islam.* Westport CT: Pir Publications.

Spelman, Elizabeth. 1988. *Inessential Woman: Problems of Exclusion in Feminist Thought.* Boston: Beacon Press.

Spivak, Gayatri. 1988. "Can the Subaltern Speak?" In Cary Nelson and Lawrence Grossberg, eds., *Marxism and the Interpretation of Culture.* Urbana: University of Illinois Press. 271-97.

Trinh, Minh-ha. 1989. *Woman, Native, Other.* Bloomington: Indiana University Press.

_____. 1991. *When the Moon Waxes Red: Representation, Gender and Cultural Politics.* New York: Routledge.

Visweswaran, Kamala. 1994. "Betrayal: An Analysis in Three Acts." In Kamala Visweswaran, ed., *Fictions of Feminist Ethnography.* Minneapolis: University of Minnesota Press. 40-59.

Wadud, Amina. 1999. *Quran and Woman: Rereading the Sacred Text from a Woman's Perspective.* New York: Oxford University Press.

Wallerstein, Immanuel. 1979. *The Capitalist World Economy.* New York: Cambridge University Press.

Wekker, Gloria. 1997. "One Finger Does Not Drink Okra Soup: Afro-Surinamese Women and Critical Agency." In Jacqui Alexander and Chandra Mohanty, eds., *Feminist Genealogies, Colonial Legacies, Democratic Futures.* New York: Routledge. 330-352.

Williams, Patricia. 1991. *The Alchemy of Race and Rights.* Cambridge, MA: Harvard University Press.

Wolf, Diane, ed. 1994. *Feminist Dilemmas in Fieldwork.* Boulder, CO: Westview.

Aunt Lute Books is a multicultural women's press that has been committed to publishing high quality, culturally diverse literature since 1982. In 1990, the Aunt Lute Foundation was formed as a non-profit corporation to publish and distribute books that reflect the complex truths of women's lives and the possibilities for personal and social change. We seek work that explores the specificities of the very different histories from which we come, and that examines the intersections between the borders we all inhabit.

Please write, phone, or e-mail (books@auntlute.com) us if you would like us to send you a free catalog of our books or if you wish to be on our mailing list for news of future titles. You may buy books from our website, by phoning in a credit card order, or by mailing a check with the catalog order form.

Aunt Lute Books

P.O. Box 410687

San Francisco, CA 94141

415.826.1300

This publication of this book would not have been possible without the kind contributions of the Aunt Lute Founding Friends:

Anonymous Donor   Diana Harris

Anonymous Donor   Phoebe Robins Hunter

Rusty Barcelo   Diane Mosbacher, M.D., Ph.D.

Marian Bremer   Sara Paretsky

Marta Drury   William Preston, Jr.

Diane Goldstein   Elise Rymer Turner